Embracing Ou

Embracing Our Mortality

*Hard Choices in an Age
of Medical Miracles*

LAWRENCE J. SCHNEIDERMAN, MD

UNIVERSITY PRESS

2008

OXFORD
UNIVERSITY PRESS

Oxford University Press, Inc., publishes works that further
Oxford University's objective of excellence
in research, scholarship, and education.

Oxford   New York
Auckland   Cape Town   Dar es Salaam   Hong Kong   Karachi
Kuala Lumpur   Madrid   Melbourne   Mexico City   Nairobi
New Delhi   Shanghai   Taipei   Toronto

With offices in
Argentina   Austria   Brazil   Chile   Czech Republic   France   Greece
Guatemala   Hungary   Italy   Japan   Poland   Portugal   Singapore
South Korea   Switzerland   Thailand   Turkey   Ukraine   Vietnam

Copyright © 2008 by Oxford University Press, Inc.

Published by Oxford University Press, Inc.
198 Madison Avenue, New York, New York 10016

www.oup.com

Oxford is a registered trademark of Oxford University Press

Library of Congress Cataloging-in-Publication Data
Schneiderman, L. J.
Embracing our mortality: hard choices in an age
of medical miracles / Lawrence J. Schneiderman.
p. ; cm.
Includes bibliographical references and index.
ISBN: 978-0-19-533945-1
1. Terminal care–Decision making.   2. Advance directives (Medical care)
3. Patient refusal of treatment.   4. Right to die.
[DNLM: 1. Terminal Care–ethics.   2. Advance Directives.
3. Bioethical Issues.   4. Medical Futility.
5. Right to Die–ethics. WB 310 S3595e 2008]   I. Title.
R726.8.S3384 2008
179.7–dc22   2007031635

1   3   5   7   9   8   6   4
Printed in the United States of America
on acid-free paper

To my patients and colleagues and the inhabitants of my library—my teachers.

Acknowledgments

Portions of this book are based on previously published articles that have been revised and updated and are cited in the References sections. I wish to express my gratitude to Holly D. Teetzel and David Strom who provided invaluable help in preparing the manuscript.

Contents

Contents

"There is a kind of striving that is appropriate to a human life; and there is a kind of striving that consists in trying to depart from that life to another life. This is what *hubris* is—the failure to comprehend what sort of life one has actually got, the failure to live within its limits (which are also possibilities), the failure, being mortal, to think mortal thoughts. Correctly understood, the injunction to avoid hubris is not a penance or denial—it is an instruction as to where the valuable things *for us* are to be found."

Martha Nussbaum, "Transcending Humanity"
in *Love's Knowledge*
(Oxford University Press, 1990), p. 381

Embracing Our Mortality

Introduction:
Facts, Statistics, Empathy
and Imagination

Much of this book is devoted to the difficult medical decisions many of us will have to make when we are seriously—possibly even terminally—ill. How dreary, you think. And yet there's a remarkable paradox: The people who have shared the kinds of experiences I will describe in this book—physicians, nurses, social workers, volunteers, and chaplains—are not dreary at all. We are, for the most part, a remarkably cheerful bunch of people who are open to so many large and small pleasures of living. Why? I think because we have come to know the alternative. Not just death, but a more inhumane form of death. Not living, but being kept alive. (I regret to say that in some of the cases I describe you'll see what I mean.)

Our feelings are not based on the banalities and false hopes that fill the books of New Age gurus (see Chapter 10). They are grounded in a deeper, more enduring, and satisfying reality. We know someday life will end. Therefore, every day, every moment, we appreciate it all the more. We enjoy the simple sensation of living as much and as long as our minds and bodies let us. In other words, we embrace our mortality.

In my 50 years of medical practice, the last 25 as a consultant in medical ethics, I've tried to help hundreds of patients, their families, and even my colleagues make the kind of tough medical decisions—the best possible decisions—I will describe in this book.

One of my patients was Amelia Briggs (her name has been changed for her privacy), a former grade school teacher in her fifties with far advanced, incurable esophageal cancer. She was finding it increasingly difficult, then impossible, to swallow food or liquids, even her saliva, which drooled foully from her swollen face. She had reached this stage after going through multiple surgical procedures and courses of radiation therapy and chemotherapy. During those years of caring for her, I had gotten to know her well. She enjoyed describing her hikes and meditations, the accomplishments of her students, and her acts of political and environmental protests. We enjoyed recommending books to each other.

She had accepted the relentless course of the disease with great dignity, understanding when friends and family no longer wanted to be with her and when the school principal called her into his office and asked her to stop teaching because her appearance was frightening the children.

At this point she was emaciated, barely able to sit up in bed, not in pain but nevertheless miserable. The next treatment choice available to her, bypassing the cancer's obstruction and eliminating the salivary downpour, would be drugs to reduce her secretions and a feeding tube inserted directly into her stomach—which would also eliminate, of course, her ability to taste whatever she ingested. This could prolong her life for several more months, perhaps. But Amelia did not wish her life to be prolonged under those circumstances. She asked me, the physician who had cared for her the longest and knew her best, to help her die peacefully. Lots of morphine could do it, but the revered and authoritative textbook of pharmacology known to all of us physicians simply as "*Goodman and Gilman*"[1] states that morphine is indicated for severe pain, not for feeling miserable. What should I do?

This is one of the classical dilemmas of modern medicine. I hope, of course, I will persuade you that I did the right thing, that the two of us made the best possible medical decision. But my justification will take you on a rather long excursion through facts, statistics, empathy, and imagination.

In a simpler time—not all that long before I entered medical school—a physician could do very little when first encountering someone like Mrs. Briggs. Both watched helplessly as the cancer invaded and disabled vital organs. The patient lived and died— just once.

Today, a moribund patient with life-threatening cancer may die a thousand times, almost literally of a thousand cuts. Today, a physician can enter the body's lumps, swellings, spots and shadows, discolorations and bleedings, not only the old-fashioned way with scalpels, scissors and steel sigmoidoscopes, urethral catheters, and vaginal speculums but far more deeply and adroitly with sinuous tubes that can be threaded through needles and weaved all the way to the depths of the heart or lungs or liver or kidneys or brain. With tubes that can illuminate the entire gastro-intestinal system from top to bottom. With tubes that carry minute hooks or scissors or needles that can pierce and extract pieces of flesh or bone or can inject fluids that are visible to X-ray machines or radioactive sensors. Physicians can supplement these with ultrasound images or with even more detailed images obtained by computerized axial tomography (CAT), magnetic resonance imaging (MRI), and positron-emission tomography (PET) scanners, to mention just a few.

In short, the entire body can be laid open for the most intimate investigations.

Physicians justify these invasive diagnostic procedures because they (and the patient with cancer) hope their discoveries will allow the patient to be hauled back from death by means of even more invasive therapeutic procedures, including radical surgeries, toxic drugs, and total body irradiation with bone marrow replacement, all the while being supported by "intensive care," including mechanical ventilation, intravenous antibiotics, renal dialysis, cardiac pumps, and pacemakers, along with oxygen and artificial nutrients and fluids.

Are all these so-called "heroic measures" worth doing? Americans certainly think so. In the United States, Intensive Care Unit (ICU) costs consume 1% of the Gross Domestic Product (GDP). (That's percentage of total GDP, not just of health-care costs.) They point to lucky friends and family members—and strangers briefly elevated to media celebrity—whose lives were "miraculously" saved and extended by years when the medical interventions occurred early enough and the type of cancer was accommodating. But the truth is that for many patients like Amelia Briggs, who have advanced metastatic cancer, these life-saving treatments provide benefits that are measured in weeks or months at most, all the while provoking waves of hope and despair through remissions and relapses.

At the end of all this hope and despair comes the inevitable finale: electric-shocking, chest-pummeling, rib-cracking efforts at cardiopulmonary resuscitation (CPR). Why inevitable? Because, having seen on television how CPR brings patients back from the brink of death, Americans prevail upon physicians to "do everything." So embedded is this last-ditch effort in our society that it is the one invasive medical intervention that legally requires no prior informed consent. *Full Code* is the default order. In many hospitals it must be done unless the patient refuses (in writing!)— or is already dead.

In the end, of course, we all die of something—if not of cancer, then of something else (heart disease, organ failure, frailty, dementia, or all of the above). More often than we would wish, we reach a point—usually in the hospital—where tough decisions have to be made.

Although most Americans say they want to die at home, 80% die in a health care setting outside the home, 60% in an acute care hospital, 20% percent in a nursing home. This means that physicians write the orders that determine how most Americans die. And, contrary to the nearly 70% success rate seen on popular television dramas,[2] attempted CPR rarely succeeds in reviving a hospitalized patient to a condition that allows the patient to leave the hospital. A bedridden patient with metastatic cancer like Amelia's has a less than 1% chance.[3] So *whether* we die in this age of miracles is not a matter of choice, only *how* we die—peacefully or badly.

Some of us have seen how the very same powers that physicians draw upon to save lives are capable of imposing terrible suffering or unwanted and meaninglessly protracted existence. We have witnessed or participated in conflicts over how to use these powers when someone we dearly love nears the end of life. These can be occasions when even the most dedicated and well-meaning physicians and family members find themselves locked in passionate exhortations on behalf of diametrically opposite courses of action. The notorious case of Terri Schiavo, a young, permanently unconscious woman whose treatment plans were fought over by her husband and parents, drawing the attention of the nation all the way up to the President, gave the public a glimpse of how vitriolic these disputes can become (see Chapter 2).

If physicians or family members insist on attempting CPR on a terminally ill patient, the price will likely be more days of misery (now with broken ribs, limbs tethered to intravenous lines, body hooked to beeping monitors, and an endotracheal tube lodged in the throat) before death comes to collect. Or, if family members call upon the physician to insert a feeding tube so their loved one (who shows no desire to eat or drink) won't die of "thirst and starvation," the patient (who, in a terminal state, is more likely experiencing no such sensations) will only be made more miserable. Because pushing hydration and liquefied food into a moribund body will likely drown the lungs and make breathing more uncomfortable, risking aspiration pneumonia and death by choking, adding to the indignities of urinary and fecal incontinence, without adding any days of life.

The media romanticize these tortuous journeys as "battles." But cancer cells are not an enemy; they are indifferent to whether or not you are "a fighter." They are only doing what nature tells them to do. Sometimes we are our own worst enemy.

During the course of her treatment, Amelia and I had already gone over a substantial array of empirical facts and statistics about cancer treatments based on rigorously conducted randomized double-blind trials. I explained how in this so-called "gold standard" of clinical research, two or more groups of patients with cancer are assigned randomly (to prevent biasing the outcomes by comparing patients with unequal risks) to different treatments. One treatment is the standard conventional treatment—or if there is no such standard, an inactive substance called a *placebo*. The other treatment is the new treatment that is "promising" based on preliminary studies.

Both the patients and the researchers are "blind" as to which treatment the patient receives (thus eliminating bias in their evaluations). After a carefully monitored period of time, the code is broken and the results analyzed to see whether one or another treatment is significantly better than the others. This information is peer-reviewed by other physician-scientists and statisticians, then published and made available to the medical community.

Based on the latest of these randomized controlled trials, a doctor may be able to tell a patient that a newly developed drug has been shown to give the average patient with a specific type of cancer at a certain stage a 20% chance of adding 40 days of life. This is a modest but statistically significant improvement over the old treatment.

Of course, that is the average (median) outcome in the patients who participated in the research trial. Half of those patients did better; half did worse—which likely will be true for any new patients taking the drug. Just as a result of random distribution—influenced almost certainly by unknown genetic or environmental factors—some patients will do better, some will do worse. That kind of information is as close to facts and statistics as the doctor can offer.

But what does one do with that information? How does one incorporate the uncertainty about days of survival into values the patient and family hold dear? How does one compare weeks or months of life with the kinds of benefits the patient may or may not be seeking? Will the "successful" treatment merely keep body parts going while the patient continues to suffer or remains insensate? How does one calculate suffering? Note that the suffering—as well as burdens and costs—will not be limited to the patient but will affect all those close to the patient: family members, lovers, intimate friends. In other words, how does one put together these facts and statistics and come up with an answer to the question: What should we do now? Where does one look for help in answering this question?

In my view we must look beyond numbers. Modern medicine has become dominated by a special kind of intellectual ritual, shaped and validated by instrumentation, quantification, replication, hard-edged activities that characterize the so-called "basic sciences." Displaced by these steely disciplines are acts of empathy and of the imagination, which are (the related word) imagistic, whether verbal, pictorial, or conceptual, which have shadows and vanishing points, coiling ambiguities, which are, in short, the stuff of what it is to be human.

These kinds of perspectives add an unsettling complexity to our quest for an answer and add a variety of new questions, all of them variations on the basic question we address in this book again and again: What should we do now?

Physicians began to ask these kinds of questions most seriously in the 1960s, when new life-saving technologies, such as kidney dialysis, CPR, organ transplantation, and intensive care units, began to make their way into hospitals. Or rather a few philosophers and theologians began to ask. Physicians soon followed. They were pioneers in a rapidly developing field called medical ethics. As early as the 1960s, but more intensively during the 1970s and 1980s, medical ethics and its practical application, medical ethics consultation, developed into a medical specialty. Soon the Joint Commission on the Accreditation of Health Care Organizations mandated that every hospital have an ethics consultation service designed to deal ethically, legally, and humanely with intractable treatment disputes.

Who were these skeptical, curious, even nosy people who called themselves medical ethics consultants? At first many physicians resented "outsiders" probing into their work (some still do), asking irritating questions that were variations on, "Why are you doing this?" Their responses always seemed to be variations on, "Because we can." In other words, medicine had become mired in what is called *the technological imperative*. If a treatment had a chance, even a minute chance, of prolonging life—no matter what condition of life, even permanently unconscious life—it was assumed to be obligatory.

Medicine had become thrall to the successes of subspecialization (which fragmented the patient into body parts) and basic science and technology (which predicted the conquest of all diseases by their methodology). Patients and loved ones, responding to the hyperbole, began to demand miracles. "*How can you be absolutely sure* [insert name of loved one here] *won't miraculously recover and walk out of here tomorrow?*" they would plead. Inevitably, this led to fierce and agonizing conflicts over "What should we do now?"

There is no question that the descendents of the scientific method have added exactitude to medical reasoning and remarkable discoveries in biology and pathology.

I remember once as an intern questioning my attending physician who had ordered that a patient be given a treatment that so far as I knew was considered useless if not harmful. "What is the evidence this treatment works?" I asked him, thinking that perhaps he was aware of better studies refuting the ones I had read. Instead, he smiled, patted me on the shoulder, and intoned patronizingly: "That is the Art of Medicine," invoking an expression made honorable by that late nineteenth- and early twentieth-century icon, Sir William Osler. But in this man's hands, the expression was a travesty. He was pretentiously pretending to know more than he did, unsupported by the slightest bit of empirical evidence. The attending physician assumed I would consider his status as sufficient authority. Instead, I concluded he was a dangerous man. From then on I became suspicious of anyone invoking that hallowed phrase, "the Art of Medicine." Long before the term became fashionable, I was a devotee of "evidence-based medicine."

But it is true, there really is an art to medicine that rewards us for paying attention to mysteries too elusive and deep for the randomized controlled trial. When people ask me, "When did you first become interested in medical ethics?" I invariably answer, "When I was a literature major in college." (Which was before the field of medical ethics even existed.) Because I came away from that time of my life—when the humanities were still revered— imbued with great writers like Tolstoy, Chekhov, Thomas Mann, George Eliot, and Saul Bellow. These were not only marvelous writers, they were brilliant observers, profound thinkers, teachers who made me aware of the deep and painful thoughts and feelings aroused by illness and death, the capriciousness of fate, the unexpected dignity in suffering, the power of simple acts of kindness, and the haunting desires and ambitions we discover in ourselves, sometimes too late and at the worst of times. Their wisdom and music remained with me throughout my medical career, even through my years of research and counseling in genetics, even while I performed highly quantitative randomized controlled clinical trials.

In other words, to really help patients and their families, I discovered I had to apply *both* the quantitative observations from empirical research and qualitative lessons from the humanities.

One day, in the spring of 1985, I decided to offer an elective course to medical students called "The Good Doctor: The Literature and Medicine of Anton Chekhov."[4] Naturally, I looked for experienced colleagues to help me. My first contact was not encouraging. A professor with expertise in Chekhov bluntly refused to have anything to do with me: "I don't want a doctor who knows Chekhov. I want a doctor who knows how to take out my appendix!" Fortunately, I was able to locate more agreeable colleagues from literature and theater. We read some of Chekhov's letters and about a dozen short stories along with the play *Cherry Orchard*, and we observed a rehearsal by graduate theater students. Once a week we sat around a table and talked. Thanks to Chekhov, I found many occasions to relate our readings to experiences I had as a physician. I also pointed out how, by selecting a few of many possible details, Chekhov makes his descriptions vivid and reveals his characters. This, I said, is what we must do as physicians: select details among the many that confront us, and find the pattern in those that reveal the diagnosis and illuminate the patient's illness and the routes to treatment.

At first, all I hoped was that the seminars would be interesting. It was not long, however, before I realized that what the students were going through was not only interesting, but important. By the end of the course I was convinced that it was not only important

13

but essential. Nowhere else in the medical curriculum did the students confront and discuss the wide array of human concerns raised by Chekhov (and by our patients).

After several years I decided to expand beyond Chekhov to include other great works of fiction as well as poetry. For example, I enjoyed comparing the tempestuous richness of Anne Sexton's "Unknown Girl in the Maternity Ward" with the terse jotting of the physician-poet William Carlos Williams' "Spring and All" (see Appendix). These poems, I tell the students, illustrate the kind of reduction that takes place between the patient's story and the medical record. It is unavoidable—medicine has to keep pace with the never-ending flow of patients and with the onrush of disease itself—but if you are really a good physician, you will, like Williams, keep the story alive, vivid, and therefore accurate.

I also liked to point out how great writers provide a descriptive precision beyond mere numbers. For example, who needs a thermometer when Shakespeare's Hamlet says, "The air bites, shrewdly; it is very cold," and Horatio replies, "It is a nipping and an eager air"?

And then there is Tolstoy's long short story "Death of Ivan Ilych"—a text many of us consider an indispensable complement to *Goodman and Gilman*—which unfolds in excruciating detail the last months, then days, then moments from the perspective of a man dying of a painful illness. Along with this imaginary man, Ivan Ilych, we experience how arrogant doctors prolonged his suffering, "tortured him" with "lies enacted over him on the eve of his death," and "degraded this awful solemn act." Along with him, we come to discover how his only source of help is the peasant, Gerasim, who comforts him by simple acts, like holding up his legs, but even more because "Gerasim did not lie."

14

Will these vicarious experiences sensitize the students to what their future patients really want? Will they make them better doctors? I confess I have no empirical evidence to support my belief that they will. And even if I did, would the barons of science who rule over today's "core curriculum" ever be persuaded to yield some of their turf?

I have my own dark image of medical education, based on the term neurologists use to describe a brain tumor growing within the confines of the skull. They call it "an expanding space occupying lesion." Gradually and inexorably, the hard tumor enlarges and crushes the soft tissue of the brain. By analogy, medical student education, since the beginning of the twentieth century, has taken place within the rigid confines of a four-year curriculum. Imagine all the discoveries in hard science that have occurred since then—in physics, physiology, molecular biology, genetics, biochemistry, pharmacology, pathology, immunology. Once upon a time, the softer humanities were part of the medical curriculum. But not anymore. The barons of science simply cannot find any room. Not surprisingly, these soft subjects have been crushed into extinction.

Why then do I continue to teach with conviction? Because I already know this much: Patients rarely speak in terms of facts and statistics, as important as they are. Indeed, numerous studies have shown that human beings have great difficulty coping with quantitative probabilities. Rather, they speak not with numbers but with words, with their own distinctive kind of literature, often in metaphors. To understand them requires empathy and imagination.

One patient of mine, an elderly, lonely man, lamented that he had "no lead in his pencil, but no one to write to anyway."

Another man wasting away slowly, who prided himself on his fruit orchard, sighed with resignation, "I can no longer reach the apricots at the tops of the trees. The story of my life."

These lines of poetry were the clues that helped me help them at the end of their life, helped me connect in their own language to their deepest fears and feelings when tough decisions had to be made, when the inevitable question came up: What should we do now? It is my hope that this book will persuade others—physicians, patients, and loved ones—to look for the revealing interplay among facts, statistics, empathy, and imagination when it is their turn to make tough decisions.

And now, after this long excursion, I bring you back to Amelia Briggs. Where did I end up after stumbling through all the facts, statistics, empathy, and imagination I tried to put to use? You can probably predict. In one respect the end was simple. Whatever you think of my actions ethically, clearly I violated the law. As I said, Amelia was not close to her family; she insisted this was to be a private matter.

After meeting with the nurses, which I continued to do every day, and after persuading the rest of the health care team, I started her on continuous intravenous morphine. She died four days later. Her last statement to me was to thank me, as much with her eyes as with her voice. There was absolutely no deception to what we were about. We would not degrade this "awful, solemn act."

Hospice calls it terminal (or nowadays, more cautiously, palliative) sedation, a treatment aimed at relief of severe pain: high doses of morphine if it is the only way possible. But you may recall, I did not have that excuse: she was not in pain, at least not the kind of pain *Goodman and Gilman* permits you to treat with morphine, although many hospices will employ the treatment for "suffering." (Which is one reason I think the hyperbolic debate over euthanasia/physician aid in dying is bogus, condemned by public figures who have never spent a day in the ICU, and performed every day by physicians.[5])

Amelia's choice to violate the law by asking me to kill her was rational and well-considered, and so was mine by acceding to her request. The U.S. Attorney General would not have approved. But I think Tolstoy, my preferred ethical mentor in this matter, would have. And all those caring for Amelia, exercising their capacity for empathy and imagination, accepted it as an act not of law but of compassion, as the best possible medical decision under the circumstances.

A word now about the book that follows: As I said at the beginning, much of it deals with the difficult medical decisions many of us will have to make when we are seriously—possibly even terminally—ill. The patients I describe range across the variety of ethnic groups that make up our country, from newborns to the elderly, including those who are rich or poor, citizens or illegal immigrants, those who are devoutly religious and those who are not. They all share one feature—they are mortal. No one has more vital body parts—heart, liver, lungs, kidneys, brain—than the other. No matter where they came from and what they believe, they are all subject to the same laws of nature. Having cared for so many, I have most profoundly learned this lesson. New discoveries will give us more choices, of course—many of them wonderful additions to medical possibilities. But, in my view, nothing will ever replace the life-enhancing value of honestly facing—and embracing—our mortality.

REFERENCES

1. Brunton L., Lazo J., Parker, K. *Goodman & Gilman's The Pharmacological Basis of Therapeutics,* 11th Ed. New York: McGraw-Hill, 2006.
2. Diem SJ, Lantos JD, Tulsky JA. Cardiopulmonary resuscitation on television. Miracles and misinformation. *New England Journal of Medicine* (1996) 334:1578–82.
3. Faber-Langendoen, Resuscitation of patients with metastatic cancer: Is transient benefit still futile? *Archives of Internal Medicine* (1991) 151:235–39.
4. Schneiderman LJ. The Good Doctor: The Literature and Medicine of Anton Chekhov (and Others). *Family Medicine* (2001) 33(1):11–13.
5. Quill TE, Battin MP. *Physician-Assisted Dying: The Case for Palliative Care & Patient Choice.* Baltimore: Johns Hopkins University Press. 2004.

CHAPTER ONE

Putting in Writing What You Want (and Don't Want)

One of my patients, Earl Adams (not his real name), an African-American in his late seventies, was afflicted with severe Parkinsonism. Not only could he no longer play the organ for Sunday church services, he could barely move and relied on his devoted wife for even the most basic needs. She got him out of bed in the morning, helped him to the toilet, bathed him, fed him, kept him upright during the day, and returned him to bed at night. So successful was she at these tasks that whenever she brought him to see me he was always clean-shaven and meticulously dressed, complete with jacket and tie.

During one of his visits, the three of us discussed his future treatment wishes if, as was inevitable, he reached a state of complete immobility. Should we insert a feeding tube if he no longer could swallow? Aggressively treat pneumonia with antibiotics, intubation, and mechanical ventilation? Or instead accept it as his terminal pneumonia (what experienced physicians have long called "the old man's friend") and make sure he dies comfortably?

What did he want us to do if he had a catastrophic event like a heart attack? Did he want us to attempt cardiopulmonary resuscitation (CPR)? Place him on a cardiac monitor and, if necessary, a cardiac pacemaker?

These were the kinds of questions I already had begun asking my elderly patients long before the federal government enacted the Patient Self-Determination Act. This Act requires that all hospitals and institutions certified by Medicare or Medicaid inform their patients about the availability of advance directives and the patients' legal right to accept or refuse medical treatment.[1]

I would explain that I wanted to know whether they had any treatment preferences they would like to inform me about in case they became very sick and were unable to participate in future decision-making. Rather than looks of outrage that I would dare suggest they might not live forever, I was answered with outbursts of relief. "Thank goodness you asked me," was the general response. Then they implored that they be allowed to die in peace and not be "hooked up" to machines. I wrote all their requests down in their medical records.

As I did for Mr. Adams. I recorded all his treatment preferences: comfort care only, no antibiotics, no ventilator, no tube feedings; in short, no aggressive life-sustaining treatments. All very well, except that the catastrophic event occurred while I was out of town for a week and he collapsed with a ruptured aortic aneurysm. This should have been his merciful death, except that Mrs. Adams panicked, dialed 911, and watched as her husband was hauled away in an ambulance—to another hospital.

All our preparations were for naught, all the carefully documented instructions reposed deep in the bowels of the medical record department—of another hospital. For a week Earl was rushed back and forth between the operating room and the Intensive Care Unit while his intimidated wife could only wring her hands helplessly. The doctors ignored her feeble protests—they had a job to do—briskly attending to his many recurrent emergency complications. It was a week before Earl died and before I heard anything about it.

I berated myself miserably, of course. What could I have done differently? There *has* to be a better way, a way for patients to ensure that their future treatment wishes are known and honored.

About the same time, in the mid-1980s, many other physicians began to express the same concerns.[2,3,4] Surely, they reasoned, if persons can retain rights over their property after death and dispose of it with estate wills, patients should not lose their rights under informed consent law to decide what is done with their own bodies before they die. This line of reasoning gave rise to documents known as advance medical directives.[5]

Although the concept of advance medical directives is a relatively new development in medical practice, its origins can be traced back to the beginning of the last century in the form of informed consent law. Courts throughout the United States have consistently and repeatedly upheld the rights of patients to be active and informed participants in their own treatment plans and to refuse unwanted treatment.[6]

As stated in the 1982 report by the President's Commission for the Study of Ethical Problems in Medicine, informed consent is "rooted in the fundamental recognition—reflected in the legal presumption of competency—that adults are entitled to accept or reject health-care interventions on the basis of their own personal values and in furtherance of their own personal goals."[7] This right to refuse any treatment—even life-sustaining medical treatment—was effectively elevated to a Constitutional principle by the U.S. Supreme Court in their 1990 decision involving a permanently unconscious young woman, Nancy Cruzan.[8]

By now every state has legalized some form of advance directive, and the documents have gained widespread professional and public endorsement.[9,10,11,12,13,14] Advance directives generally consist of either one or both of two components: a proxy directive (Durable Power of Attorney for Health Care), which allows you to designate a surrogate decision maker in the event you lose decision-making capacity, and an instruction directive (Living Will), which provides space for you to specify treatments, such as CPR, mechanical ventilation, or tube feeding, that you would or would not want in given clinical circumstances.[5]

Unfortunately, researchers were just beginning to explore the best ways to implement these advance directives when the concept was precipitously turned into federal legislation in 1991 under the Patient Self-Determination Act.[1]

Why do I say "unfortunately" and "precipitously"? Because at the time of its enactment we had no idea whether these documents actually would be useful. No empirical studies had been carried out regarding their effect on medical practice and outcomes, nor did Congress provide any guidelines for carrying out the Act's intent, nor include any funding provisions or evaluation component. Even now there is little empirical evidence supporting their validity, reliability, or effectiveness. The Act became another unproven, unfunded—and often only grudgingly accepted—governmental mandate.

For example, many hospitals have chosen the easiest, least costly way to comply with the letter of the law. During administrative processing at hospital admission, the patient is handed boilerplate documents referring to the state's position on advance directives. In other words, a clerk, in the midst of discussing payment and insurance details with a patient or family, is the person assigned the delicate task of seeking the patient's preference for CPR and other life-sustaining interventions.

And now for some facts and statistics. You already may have definite ideas about what you want and don't want. For example, a 1985 Harris poll indicated that 85% of Americans endorsed the statement, "A patient with a terminal disease ought to be able to tell his doctors to let him die when there is no cure in sight."[25] Nevertheless, only about 10% of Americans, healthy or ill, have actually expressed those wishes in an advance directive. Although these completion rates can be improved by efforts at education and encouragement, they rarely rise to more than 20%. Our own efforts, in which physicians underwent training sessions on offering advance directives, with follow-up carried out by dedicated researchers, are almost alone in achieving a completion rate greater than 50%.[26,27,28]

In one study we interviewed over 100 seriously ill patients with cancer and their physicians and discovered that most physicians were unaware of their patients' wishes.[29] Less than one-third of the patients claimed that they had any discussion of treatment decisions with their physicians. And even these discussions were general and not directed specifically at whether or not to provide tube feedings or mechanical ventilation, or to attempt CPR.

In another study involving patients with severe life-threatening illness, such as cancer, heart disease, pulmonary disease, and AIDS, these documents were rarely called upon at critical decision-making times.[26] In this study we hoped to show that encouraging patients to execute advance directives would not only enhance their role in decision making, but also, by eliminating unwanted expensive end-of-life treatments, would provide a more acceptable way to reduce health-care costs than imposing rationing. The results proved our hopes to be unfounded—the use of advance directives did not reduce health-care costs.

So why bother with advance directives? Here I want to make clear that despite these problems, and even more serious problems I will mention later, I believe that everyone is better served with such a document than without one.

For one thing, advance directives provide the strongest grounds for assuring your doctors that a proxy decision maker (whom you have chosen) is acting in accordance with what you would want for yourself. This process is called *substituted judgment.* If you were unable to communicate your wishes because you were seriously ill or unconscious, your physicians, after describing the clinical circumstances and prognosis, would quite reasonably ask someone who knows you well (e.g., an intimate friend, a spouse, or family member) whether they thought you would want CPR attempted in the event of cardiac arrest.

The physicians appropriately want to know not what *they* (i.e., your spouse, friend, or family member) would want, but what *you* would want. Their responses would necessarily be based on substituted judgment, namely, their familiarity with *your* values and goals as it would apply to this particular set of circumstances. Being the agent named in an advance directive carries decisive weight whenever a dispute occurs over end-of-life medical treatment decisions. Many family members have told me and my research assistants that having such a document in hand gave them a sense of power they would not ordinarily feel in the intimidating hospital setting.

24

Unfortunately, substituted judgment is not perfect. Researchers have discovered that spouses, family members, and physicians, even those with years of familiarity with the patient, do a poor job of predicting what that patient would want in various end-of-life circumstances.[15,16,17,18,19,20,21,22,23] Moreover, in our own studies, we discovered that physicians unconsciously project their own values on their perceptions of what their patients would want.[30,31]

The instruction directive—commonly called a living will—also has its limits. First, its language is set at the time it is written and, thus, presents a person with the difficulty of attempting to describe within the space of a page or two what he or she would wish under a whole host of unpredictable future circumstances. As a result, instruction directives are often couched in vague all-embracing terms that are vulnerable to variable interpretations, such as "excessive burdens," "heroic measures," and "quality of life." Because patients usually lack understanding of specific complex procedures, they would not ordinarily be able to judge the indications, benefits, or risks of the many procedures they might face.[24]

Furthermore, a patient's clinical condition is not usually static; thus, it would not be unreasonable in the course of an illness for you to change your mind about life-saving treatments. Fear, pain, or a sense of hopelessness might cause you to temporarily resist highly promising resuscitative measures. Conversely, after experiencing the relentless progression of a burdensome disease, you might begin to have different thoughts about life prolongation.

Although you are not required to have legal documents or indeed any written declaration to refuse unwanted treatments, I believe that having such a document available in a central location is probably a good idea, given the nature of today's medical care system, which involves a multitude of physicians converging on

25

the patient at different times. Several excellent guides to advance care planning, including *Your Life Your Choices* and *Hard Choices for Loving People*, are available on the Internet.[32,33]

There is one observation you should be aware of, however: in our studies we found that every time a patient was hospitalized, the advance directive remained buried in the medical record room with the old records and did not make it into the active medical record. It is important, therefore, that you or your surrogate makes sure that the current advance directive is either in the active medical record or readily accessible on the hospital computer every time you are hospitalized. (As further assurance, if you have reached a stage in your illness when you are certain you do not want certain life-sustaining treatments like CPR, you can write those instructions—signed and dated—on a card you carry in your wallet. I regret not having thought of that with Earl Adams.)

Another discovery we made is that when patients give themselves time to think about these matters, they show a greater regard for others than they are given credit for.[34] For example, when we asked seriously ill patients with cancer and AIDS how much of their life savings they would be willing to spend if they were totally dependent on others for care, more than 75% expressed a wish to put some limit on their expenditures. Only 23% of the respondents claimed they would be willing to spend their entire life savings. A larger proportion (27%) said that they would not wish to spend any of their life savings.

When we asked the same patients what they would want if they were totally dependent on family and friends for care, over 85% stated a preference for some limitation on how long they would want to live in that condition. Only 14%said that they would want to live as long as possible. Nearly twice that many (28%)

stated that they did not want to live at all under such circumstances, and 60% stated that they would want to live no longer than 30 days.

One observation was perhaps counterintuitive, given all that is "known" about gender stereotypes (e.g., that "nurturing" women would be more likely to yield to the pressures of limiting their life-sustaining treatments): Among patients with cancer, women were willing to spend an average of 22% more of their life savings than men, and a larger percentage of women than men expressed a desire to live as long as possible (27% compared to 14%).

Despite all the efforts to encourage the public to complete advance directives, there seems to be an irreducible core of patients who refuse to do so, who seem to be psychologically resistant to communicating—or even considering—their end-of-life treatment wishes. Along with Woody Allen, they appear to be saying: "I'm not afraid of death. I just don't want to be there when it happens." Are you one of them?

In the next chapter, we will see what can happen when a dispute arises and you have not made your treatment wishes known in a way that is "clear and convincing."

REFERENCES

1. Omnibus Reconciliation Act 1990. Title IV. Section 4206. *Congressional Record*, October 26, 1990:12,638.
2. Bedell SE, Delbanco TL. Choices about cardiopulmonary resuscitation in the hospital: When do physicians talk with patients? *New England Journal of Medicine* (1984) 310: 1089–93.
3. Shmerling RH, Bedell, Lilienfeld A, et al. Discussing cardiopulmonary resuscitation: a study of elderly outpatients. *Journal of General Internal Medicine* (1988) 3: 317–21.

4. Bedell SE, Pelle D, Majer PL, et al. Do-not-resuscitate order for critically ill patients in the hospital. How are they used and what is their impact? *Journal of the American Medical Association* (1986) 256: 233–7.

5. Schneiderman LJ, Arras JD. Counseling patients to counsel physicians on future care in the event of patient incompetence. *Annals of Internal Medicine* (1985) 102: 603–8.

6. *Pratt v. Carvalho*, 118 Ill. App. 161, 166 (1905), aff'd, 244 Ill. 30, 79 N.E. 562 (1906); *Schloendorff v. New York Hospital*, 211 N.Y. 127, 129, 105 N.E. 92, 93 (1914); *Salgo v. Leland Stanford Jr. University Board of Trustees*, 154 Cal. App. 2d 560, 317 P. 2d 170 (1957); *Cobbs v. Grant*, 8 Cal. 3d 229, 502 P. 2d 1 (1972); *Canterbury v. Spence*, 464 F. 2d 772 (D.C. Circ. 1972), *cert. denied*, 409 U.S. 1064 (1972).

7. *President's Commission for the Study of Ethical Problems in Medicine and Biomedical and Behavioral Research, Making Health Care Decisions.* (Washington, D.C., Government Printing Office, 1982), at 2–3.

8. *Cruzan v. Director*, 497 U.S. 261, 277 (1990).

9. Brunetti LL, Carperos SD, Westlund RE. Physicians' attitudes towards living wills and cardiopulmonary resuscitation. *Journal of General Internal Medicine* (1991) 6: 323–9

10. Davidson KW, Hackler C, Caradine DR, et al. Physicians' attitudes on advance directives. *Journal of the American Medical Association* (1989) 262: 2415–9.

11. Emanuel LL, Barry MJ, Stoeckle JD, et al. Advance directives for medical care—a case for greater use. *New England Journal of Medicine* (1991) 324: 889.

12. Joos SK, Reuler JB, Powell JL, Hickam DH. Outpatients' attitudes and understanding regarding living wills. *Journal of General Internal Medicine* (1993) 8: 259–63.

13. Finucane TE, Shumway JM, Powers RL, et al. Planning with elderly outpatients for contingencies of severe illness: a survey and clinical trial. *Journal of General Internal Medicine* (1988) 3: 322–5.

14. Lo B, McLeod GA, Saika G. Patient attitudes to discussing life-sustaining treatment. *Archives of Internal Medicine* (1986) 146: 1613–5.

15. Starr TJ, Pearlman RA, Uhlman RF. Quality of life and resuscitation decisions in elderly patients. *Journal of General Internal Medicine* (1986) 1: 373–9.

16. Hare J, Pratt C, Nelson C. Agreement between patients and their self-selected surrogates on difficult medical decisions. *Archives of Internal Medicine* (1992) 152: 1049–54.

17. Seckler AB, Meier DE, Mulvihill M, Cammper Paris BE. Substituted judgment: how accurate are proxy decisions? *Annals of Internal Medicine* (1991) 115: 92–8.

18. Uhlmann RF, Pearlman RA, Cain KC. Physicians' and spouses' predictions of elderly patients' resuscitation preferences; *Journal of Gerontology* (1988) 43: M115: 121.

19. Zweibel NR, Cassel CK. Treatment choices at the end of life: A comparison of decisions by older patients and their physician-selected proxies. The *Gerontoloist* (1989) 29: 615–21.

20. Diamond EL, Jernigan JA, Moseley RA, et al. Decision-making ability and advance directive preferences in nursing home patients and proxies. *The Gerontologist* (1989) 29: 622–6.

21. Sulmasy DP, Haller K, Terry PB. More talk, less paper: predicting the accuracy of substituted judgments. *American Journal of Medicine* (1994) 96: 432–8.

22. Ditto PH, Danks JH, Smucker WD, et al. Advance directives as acts of communication: a randomized controlled trial. *Archives of Internal Medicine* (2001) 161:421–30.

23. Shalowitz DI, Garrett-Mayer E, Wendler D. The accuracy of surrogate decision makers: a systematic review. *Archives of Internal Medicine* (2006) 166: 493–7.

24. Schneiderman LJ, Pearlman RA, Kaplan RM, Anderson JP, Rosenberg EM. Relationship of general advance directive instructions to specific

life-sustaining treatment preferences in patients with serious illness. *Archives of Internal Medicine* (1992) 152: 2114–22.

25. Taylor H. Withholding and withdrawal of life support from the critically ill. *New England Journal of Medicine* (1990) 322: 1891–92.

26. Schneiderman LJ, Kronick R, Kaplan RM, Anderson JP, Langer RD. Effects of offering advance directives on medical treatments and costs: a prospective study. *Annals of Internal Medicine* (1992) 1176: 599–606.

27. Molloy DW, Guyatt GH, Russo R, et al. Systematic implementation of an advance directive program in nursing homes: a randomized controlled trial. *Journal of the American Medical Association* 2000; 283: 1437–44.

28. Heiman H, Bates DW, Fairchild D, Shaykevich S, Lehmann LS. Improving completion of advance directives in the primary care setting: a randomized controlled trial. *American Journal of Medicine* (2004) 117: 318–24.

29. Virmani J, Schneiderman LJ, Kaplan RM. Relationship of advance directives to physician-patient communication. *Archives of Internal Medicine* (1994) 154: 909–13.

30. Schneiderman LJ, Kaplan RM, Pearlman RA, Teetzel H. Do physicians' own preferences for life-sustaining treatment influence their perceptions of patients' preferences. *Journal of Clinical Ethics* (1993) 4: 28–33;

31. Schneiderman LJ, Kaplan RM, Rosenberg E, Teetzel H. Do Physicians' Own Preferences for Life-Sustaining Treatment Influence Their Perceptions of Patients' Preferences? A Second Look. *Cambridge Quarterly of Healthcare Ethics* (1997) 6: 131–37.

32. *Your Life Your Choices:* Planning for Future Medical Decisions; How to Prepare a Personalized Living Will. http://www1.va.gov/hsrd/publications/internal/ylyc.pdf;

33. Dunn, H. *Hard Choices for Loving People.* http://www.hardchoices.com

34. Schneiderman LJ, Kronick R, Kaplan RM, Anderson JP, Langer RD. Attitudes of Seriously Ill Patients Toward Treatment That Involves High Costs and Burdens on Others. *Journal of Clinical Ethics* (1994) 5(2): 109–12.

CHAPTER TWO

What May Happen
If You Don't Make It
"Clear and Convincing"

Every now and then conflicts about the treatment wishes of a patient burst beyond the boundaries of the intimate doctor–patient relationship into the public arena. I will describe two such patients. One of these, Robert Wendland, became a victim of the California State Supreme Court.[1] Another patient, Terri Schiavo, more catastrophically became an involuntary performer in a nationwide political circus.[2]

Judges will confess that they abhor becoming involved in these sorts of conflicts. But what can they do? If physicians, family members, and consultants cannot decide whether to sustain aggressive life-sustaining treatments or exchange them for comfort care measures, who can? If the case is brought to court, it is, of course, judges who must. Like Robert Frost's notion of home, as "the place where if you have to go there, They have to take you in," courts play the role of last resort. If a conflict cannot be settled elsewhere, then they have to take it in.

Politicians, on the other hand, have no such excuse, and their callous, not to mention unconstitutional, intrusion into the medical and legal deliberations involving Terri Schiavo outraged the public.

First, a disclaimer: In my criticism of the unanimous decision handed down by the California State Supreme Court in the first case I will discuss, that of Robert Wendland, I must acknowledge my limited exposure to the law. It has been almost entirely case by case rather than lecture by lecture. I have never attended law school, although I have audited a few law school courses. The only expertise I can claim in matters like these is that of a physician and ethics consultant who has been involved in hundreds of bedside conflicts involving critically ill patients. In other words, real cases with all their messy humanity and rawness rather than finely polished hypotheticals.

It is obvious then that I have arrived at my perspective on the law, for the most part, from the outside and on a need-to-know basis whenever judges (and, of course, lawyers) have become involved in these bedside dramas. Nevertheless, it has not stopped me from making the following admittedly presumptuous, and perhaps misguided, observations.

My first observation comes out of my experiences with severely disabled infants at a children's hospital. Several were extremely low-birth-weight newborns who had been "miraculously rescued" and now languished in a state of miserable dependence on high technology in the Intensive Care Unit (ICU). (One unforgettable patient, a battered infant, will be described further in Chapter 8.) In all these cases, when a judge was called on to resolve a dispute over treatment, the judge appointed a guardian who invariably insisted that life-sustaining treatment be continued.

33

The judge never saw the patient, never followed up on the consequences of the decision, and never inquired about the patient again. Meanwhile it was left to the doctors and nurses to deal with the consequences of the judicial decision and experience the daily anguish of continuing the futile treatment, which led me to realize one important difference between decision-making by doctors and that of judges.

Doctors, good doctors that is, seek to base their treatment decisions on empirical evidence. They want to know outcomes; they want to know what will work. This, of course, is the foundation for medical standards of practice. Judges, on the other hand, have inherited the system of English Common Law and, for the most part, base their decisions on precedents. In medical matters, as in other matters, they seek to apply the law based on judgments reached in similar cases from the past.[3] Or they try to decipher what was intended in the language of legislative statutes.[4] They look back rather than ahead. That is their standard of practice.

Another difference became repeatedly apparent—the difference in power. No matter how vigorously physicians and medical ethicists argue and appeal to reason, compassion, what have you, we can call on nothing more than our power to persuade. Judges, meanwhile, can call on the full and many powers of society to enforce compliance with their decisions.

In the discussion that follows, I will not refer to the abstract ideals of Medicine and the Law, but rather to human actors, the fallible agents of these abstract ideals—physicians, patients, family members, medical ethicists, lawyers, and judges. All of us seek to—in fact, may honestly believe we do—act on behalf of principles. But in my view, when we gather at the patient's bedside, immersed in the dilemmas and conflicts, we rarely act as agents of principle but rather as characters in a drama. What we consider to be principled actions, pursued with all due deliberation, are inevitably mixed and stirred with the many things that make us who we are: temperament, emotions, happy and unhappy experiences, religion, social status, culture, unrecognized prejudices, and so on.

And now to the case of Robert Wendland. (All the quotations come from the California Supreme Court decision.[1])

Mr. Wendland was a 42-year-old man who, on September 29, 1993, while drunk, rolled and crashed his truck at high speed. The man remained unconscious until January 1995—some 15 months later—when, according to court testimony, his wife Rose "first noticed signs of responsiveness." From then on he remained in what is categorized as the "minimal conscious state." In other words, he was not completely unconscious (therefore impervious to pain and suffering); rather, his condition could be considered even worse—"severe cognitive impairment" along with "agitation, aggressiveness, noncompliance, incontinence of bowel and bladder, severe paralysis on the right side of his body, moderate paralysis on the left, severe swallowing dysfunction, dysphoria, spasticity, severely impaired communication, complete dependence on enteral feeding." On four occasions Mr. Wendland tore out a percutaneous endoscopic gastrostomy (PEG) tube that had been surgically implanted through his abdominal wall directly into his stomach—his sole source of nourishment. His wife, Rose, who remained devoted to his care through the entire course of his incapacity, authorized three surgical replacements. But on July, 1995—now nearly three years after his accident—following discussions with her daughters and the patient's brother, all of whom agreed that Robert "would not have approved the procedure even if necessary to sustain his life," Rose refused authorization for the fourth replacement.

They based their decision on the grounds of substituted judgment (see Chapter 1), citing statements made by Robert, such as "Don't let them do that to me," when his brother warned him of the chance of injuring himself so severely while driving in a drunken condition that he would end up lying in bed "just like a vegetable." His daughters testified that their father had told them: "If he could not do basic things, feeding himself, talking, communicating, he would not want to live." The hospital ethics committee unanimously agreed with the decision.

But at that point in stepped Mr. Wendland's estranged mother Florence and half-sister Rebekah (both of whom had long despised Mr. Wendland's wife). They obtained a temporary restraining order to bar the removal of the feeding tube. To counter their efforts, Rose, his wife of 15 years, asked for and received an appointment as his conservator. She was prohibited, however, from discontinuing his tube feedings. The PEG tube was reinserted and maintained throughout the subsequent 5 years of litigation.

At the first trial, the judge (who, the record states, "visited Robert in the hospital") ruled that Rose Wendland had not shown by clear and convincing evidence that under the circumstances her husband would want to die, nor that it was in his best interests. This decision was reversed by the Court of Appeals, which ruled that the trial court judge had erred and that the trial court's role was "merely to satisfy itself that the conservator had considered the conservatee's best interests in good faith ..." This decision, in turn, was appealed to the California Supreme Court, which on August 9, 2001, unanimously reversed the latter decision. (These justices, rather than visiting the patient, viewed a videotape that was already several years old and no longer representative of the severity of Mr. Wendland's deterioration.)

By then a large contingent of medical ethicists (including me) had joined in an amicus brief to support Rose Wendland. To no avail. The Supreme Court Justices agreed with Mr. Wendland's mother that he had never provided "clear and convincing evidence" that he would want to have his feeding tube removed while he was in "these exact circumstances," nor that discontinuing the tube feeding was in his best interests.

In their written decision the justices defined what they meant by clear and convincing evidence of the patient's wishes:

"Only when the patient's prior statements clearly illustrate a serious, well thought out, consistent decision to refuse treatment under these exact circumstances, or circumstances highly similar to the current situation, should treatment be refused or withdrawn."

With respect to his best interests, the justices were unwilling to give specific examples of what they would have accepted as clear and convincing evidence, but unanimously (and to my mind, incomprehensively) agreed that the "subjective judgment" of the woman married to Mr. Wendland for (by this time) 20 years would not suffice.

As they wrote:

"We need not in this case attempt to define the extreme factual predicates that, if proved by clear and convincing evidence, might support a conservator's decision that

37

withdrawing life support would be in the best interest of a conscious conservatee." . . . "The conservator offered no basis . . . other than her own subjective judgment that the conservatee did not enjoy a satisfactory quality of life and legally insufficient evidence to the effect that he would have wished to die."

The justices gave passing acknowledgement of the "high evidentiary burden" that would "frustrate many genuine treatment desires—particularly the choices of young people, who are less likely than older people to envision the need for advanced directives, or poor people who are less likely than affluent people to have the resources to obtain formal legal documents."

They then went on to say that this problem was easily resolved:

"The legislature has already accommodated this concern in large part by permitting patients to nominate surrogate decision makers by orally informing a supervising physician and by giving effect to specific oral health care instructions."

Unfortunately the justices seemed to know little about the reality of human behavior in these matters. In fact, most people would not be helped by the legislature's "accommodation." As we have previously noted, few people have considered, much less communicated, their health-care wishes in advance. And even if they had conveyed their instructions, either orally or by means of a document, not many laypersons have the knowledge or foresight to express their end-of-life wishes in exact detail and anticipate "exact circumstances." One entire group, the developmentally disabled from birth or childhood, could never meet the standard. As for Robert Wendland, by the time he was under medical care, he was incapable of nominating a surrogate decision maker or orally informing his supervising physician about his "specific health-care instructions."

Even while rejecting the argument that Rose Wendland had determined the conservatee's best interest "in good faith," the justices wrote:

> "The conservator shall make the decision in accordance with the conservator's determination of the conservatee's best interest. In determining the conservatee's best interest, the conservator shall consider the conservatee's personal values to the extent known to the conservator." It must be a "good faith" decision "based on medical advice."

However, the justices chose a standard of proof that was, for all practical purposes, an insurmountable barrier for Rose Wendland. Substituted judgment rests on the legal foundation that a person's body and property are inviolate and should be invaded only with the person's informed consent.[5–7] The justices demanded that such consent had to have been somehow conveyed to Mr. Wendland's wife in anticipation of "exact" and "highly similar" circumstances. Indeed, the justices found reassurance in similar decisions reached in three other states that imposed "a high standard of proof,"[8–10] and in the U.S. Supreme Court, which ruled that states may require any standard of proof they wish.[11]

By contrast, best interest is called on when the person lacks the mental capacity to give such informed consent, either personally or through a proxy. It is the standard used when weighing decisions involving children and the mentally disabled. In my view, it should have been the standard called on in this case.

Requiring Rose Wendland to produce statements by her husband that "clearly illustrate a serious, well thought out, consistent decision to refuse treatment under these exact circumstances, or circumstances highly similar to the current situation," would merely promote an absurd legal fiction. It is unrealistic. Something physicians know and judges either do not know or do not want to acknowledge: people almost never provide that kind of evidence. Moreover, it was completely unnecessary, since Rose Wendland was more than merely a court-appointed conservator; she was a manifestly devoted wife who, according to any reasonable observer, was making "a 'good faith' best interest decision 'based on medical advice.'" Is it not far more likely that any decision she made on behalf of her husband would be more wise, compassionate, loving, and in keeping with his wishes and best interests than a decision prompted by an estranged family member and rendered by "impartial" judges?

But there you have it. The justices ruled, and the feeding tube remained. Removing the tube and allowing comfort care to proceed to the end of Robert Wendland's life, regarded by his medical caretakers as a compassionate act, was deemed by the justices to be a criminal act.

Another point worth noting is that the justices seemed to have a cramped view of best interests that can only be explained by their limited knowledge of medical reality:

"An incompetent and uncommunicative but conscious conservatee might perceive the efforts to keep him alive as unwanted intrusion and the withdrawal of those efforts as welcome release. But the decision to treat is reversible. The decision to withdraw treatment is not."

In other words, prolonging conscious life in any state of suffering—even "unwanted" life—always takes precedence over the "welcome release" from that suffering. The justices further, and even perversely, elaborated on this view when they explained that their rigorous standard of proof applied only to patients under a conservatorship and allowed that they would not have been so hard to please if Robert Wendland were completely and permanently unconscious.

As they wrote:

"Our decision today affects only a narrow class of persons: conscious conservatees who have not left formal directions for health care and whose conservators propose to withhold life-sustaining treatment for the purpose of causing their conservatees' deaths. Our conclusion does not affect permanently unconscious patients, including those who are comatose or in a persistent vegetative state."

Therefore, minimal consciousness—with suffering—must be sustained; unconsciousness—with no suffering—need not be sustained. (Had Rose Wendland not been so devoted, she might have called for the withdrawal of the feeding tube after her husband had been unconscious for a year, when he fit into the diagnostic category of permanent vegetative state. Apparently the Supreme Court judges would have agreed with her at that time. Unfortunately, she waited too long.)

Robert Wendland continued to deteriorate and died of pneumonia on July 17, 2001, nearly 8 years after his injury. Although the California Supreme Court was not required to rule on the case because its ruling was mooted by Mr. Wendland's death, the court chose to issue their opinion anyway on August 9.

And now we move on to an event that became a major preoccupation of the entire country (as well as other countries), including the courts, the media, the Florida legislature and governor, Congress, and even the President of the United States—the case of Terri Schiavo. Before it was over, the Florida House and Senate had passed the first "Terri's Law," a bill (quickly ruled unconstitutional) authorizing the governor to override a court decision and replace her feeding tube; the U. S. Congress had met in a special emergency session for the first time in history to pass legislation directing the medical care of a single patient; the insensate woman had been issued an absurd subpoena to testify before a Congressional committee; the Senate leader, a physician, had rendered an incompetent diagnostic opinion on the Senate floor, based on his brief review of a videotape (an act of malpractice that may not have violated Senatorial standards, but it certainly violated medical standards); the President had hurriedly flown by helicopter into the Capitol to sign a second "Terri's Law," which attempted to override all the previous legal decisions; the Department of Children and Families attempted to seize the patient based on allegations of abuse; and appeals to the U. S. Supreme Court were rejected—all in full view of the public by means of round-the-clock sensationalized national television.

It all began when Michael Schiavo awoke to find his 25-year-old wife Terri unconscious and gasping for air. She had undergone cardiac arrest. Emergency medical technicians were called, but restoring a normal cardiac rhythm—and therefore effective blood flow to the brain—turned out to be long and difficult. Her blood tests revealed a very low serum potassium, which undoubtedly was the cause of her cardiac arrest and was thought to have resulted from erratic eating habits in her efforts to lose weight. Terri never regained consciousness and lapsed into what is called a *persistent vegetative state.* (If this form of persistent vegetative state lasts longer than 3 months, it is called *permanent vegetative state.* Terri Schiavo remained unconscious for over 15 years.)

Here a brief explanation is in order. The cerebral cortex is the portion of our brain that controls the qualities that make us who we are: our thoughts, emotions, behavior, memory, and our capacity to experience and communicate. It is a structure no thicker than a flannel cloth on the outer margin of our cerebral hemispheres. It is so sensitive to lack of oxygen that if normal heartbeat—and effective blood flow—is not restored within 4 to 6 minutes, the function of this structure is completely and permanently destroyed.

By contrast, the more primitive portion of our brain, the brain stem, controls our physiologic functions like heartbeat, respiration, swallowing, and peristalsis. It also controls our sleep–wake cycles. More hardy than the cerebral cortex, the brain stem can survive up to 15 to 20 minutes without blood-borne oxygen.

The tragedy of patients like Terri Schiavo lies within this gap of time. Even if an emergency team responds remarkably swiftly to a 911 call and resuscitates a silent heart in 10 minutes, it is already too late to save the cerebral cortex. The only part of the brain the team has rescued is the brain stem. What is particularly devastating to loved ones is that this person, whose cerebral cortex has been obliterated and who is therefore permanently unconscious, can *appear* to wake up in about a week or so when the brain stem, which has been only temporarily damaged in that gap of time, recovers. This "miracle" has often been reported in the press, then never followed up. From then on, the person maintains sleep–wake cycles. The eyes may react reflexively to sound and light, but they recognize nothing. In fact, autopsy revealed that the portion of Terri Schiavo's brain that permitted sight was destroyed. The woman who, on video clips, appeared to be casting loving glances at her mother was completely blind.

In 1992, soon after Terri's husband won a large malpractice award, he had a falling out with her parents, Robert and Mary Schindler, regarding her treatments. After initially pursuing every possible cure, including flying her across the country for a "deep brain stimulator" (which had no effect) and aggressive efforts to provide speech and physical therapy, Michael, after more than 8 years had passed, filed a petition for the court to determine whether his permanently unconscious wife's feeding tube should be removed. Based on statements his wife had made to him, to his brother, and to his sister-in-law, Michael claimed, and the trial court concurred, that his wife would not wish to be kept alive under her current circumstances and would want the feeding tube removed.

The Schindlers' opposed this decision and launched a prolonged battle that went back and forth for another 8 years through the courts, the Florida governor's office, the halls of Congress, and even to the desk of the President of the United States. It became the most extensively litigated medical trial in the history of the United States, involving repeated motions, decisions, appeals, and trials. The insensate patient was the subject of heated debates in the media by a mix of a few experts who knew what they were talking about and a much larger contingent of impassioned commentators who did not and who made false and outrageous claims about the woman's condition and prognosis.

Physicians who testified that their quack remedies would cure Terri Schiavo were summarily discredited by the presiding judge when they failed to produce any supporting evidence. The battle continued via rival Web sites and videotapes. The Schindlers' Web site showed, with great emotional impact, snippets of the videotaped neurological exam that seemed to portray Terri Schiavo smiling and recognizing her mother. Ironically, these same videotapes when viewed in their entirety, without misleading segments excerpted, provided convincing evidence to the judges that she was completely unresponsive.

Finally, 15 years after Terri Schiavo lost consciousness, the terrible circus came to an end. Her feeding tube was removed, and she died in a hospice setting 13 days later, peacefully and with no evidence of suffering. On her tombstone, Michael Schiavo, had this engraved under her name:

> "Born December 3, 1963
> Departed This Earth February 25, 1990
> At Peace March 31, 2005
> I Kept My Promise"

Is there anything we can do to protect ourselves and our loved ones from these travesties?

One problem, of course, is that most people (including Robert Wendland and Terri Schiavo) simply have not communicated their end-of-life treatment wishes in unambiguous detail. This could be particularly serious if friends and family members fight among themselves as to who is entitled to speak on behalf of the patient. In these circumstances the law can be hard, even harsh, if comfort care rather than aggressive life-sustaining treatment is being proposed. Judges seem to be moving toward requiring that the unreasonable "clear and convincing" standard of evidence be met: Did the patient's prior statements clearly illustrate a serious, well-thought-out, consistent decision to refuse treatment under these exact circumstances or circumstances highly similar to the current situation? As I noted in Chapter 1, the best protection, with all its flaws, is an advance directive, both surrogate and instruction.

Physicians also have a responsibility. Our studies have shown that they could do a much better job introducing their patients to advance care planning. In particular, physicians should not miss the many opportunities to engage their patients with chronic illness in discussions about treatments near the end of life and record the patient's wishes in the medical record. Just because a patient may lack decision-making capacity when end-of-life critical decisions must be made does not mean that treating physicians are unaware of the patient's previously expressed attitudes toward life-sustaining treatments and comfort care. Most patients with progressive terminal illness (e.g., metastatic cancer, chronic obstructive pulmonary disease, and advanced congestive heart failure) have already provided clues to their treatment wishes during the course of their illness.

Unfortunately, most patients enter the Intensive Care setting into the care of complete strangers who have no such information. Given these limitations, I always encourage critical care physicians to try to take advantage of any small window of opportunity to ask the patient for and record the name of the designated decision-maker as soon as possible at time of hospital admission.

At the same time, it is important not to over-interpret the trend toward clear and convincing evidence. The California justices stated that they intended the clear and convincing standard to apply only to the withdrawal of life-sustaining treatment by conservators (i.e., when the court is involved), not to the other "vast majority of health care decisions." As I said, judges really don't want to deal with what they regard as medical decisions. So, where there is agreement between the patient's family and the physicians, there need be no fear or hesitancy to act in the most appropriate and compassionate manner. On the other hand, if there is disagreement over treatment, it is best to have a hospital policy with explicit definitions and processes regarding life-sustaining treatments, palliative care, treatment withdrawal, and medical futility, along with a functioning ethics consultation service (see Chapter 8).

Finally—What can you do? To balance the power of judges, who have shown themselves capable of inflicting cruel and unusual punishment on patients, if not on criminals, those of you who are a trusted surrogate at the bedside of a future Robert Wendland and Terri Schiavo should be aware that if there are family conflicts, and a treatment withdrawal decision is challenged in court by anyone with standing (a spouse or blood relative)—someone who may not have seen the patient for years, even someone who has become estranged from the patient—the judge may require witnessed statements by the patient according to the clear and convincing standard. Make sure you know exactly what that means, that it is imperative that "the patient's prior statements clearly illustrate a serious, well thought out, consistent decision to refuse treatment under these exact circumstances, or circumstances highly similar to the current situation." Then reflect on and "reconsider" carefully what the patient might have told you. Be prepared to report that testimony. Clearly and convincingly.

Let *me* be clear. Lawyers (as officers of the court) are not permitted to tell their clients to lie; physicians are under no such obligation. Therefore, if the courts demand what, in my opinion, is an impossible standard of evidence and the physician feels that this impossible standard will force treatments that violate the patient's previously expressed wishes or the physician's duty of beneficence, then the physician should advise the surrogate to be sure to polish his or her recollections of the patient's previous statements in a manner that serves the patient rather than the court. I have no doubt some will find this position controversial.

REFERENCES

1. *Conservatorship of Wendland* (2001) 26 Cal. 4th 519, Aug. 9, 2001. No. S087265.
2. Cranford R. Facts, lies, and videotapes: the permanent vegetative state and the sad case of Terri Schiavo. *Journal of Law Medicine & Ethics.* (2005) 33(2): 363–71.
3. e.g, *MC, Re* [2003] QGAAT13.
4. e.g., *Gardner; re* BWV 2003 VSC 173.
5. *Union Pacific Railway Co. v. Botsford* (1891) 141 U.S. 250, 251.
6. *Schloendorff v. Society of New York Hospital* (N.Y. 1914) 105 N.E. 92,93.
7. *Cobbs v. Grant* (1972) 8 Cal. 3d 229, 242.
8. *In re Martin* (Mich. 1995) 538 N.W.2d 399.

9. *Matter of Edna* M.F. (Wis. 1997) 563 N.W.2d 485, 490.
10. *Matter of Conroy* (N.J. 1985) 486 A.2d 1209.
11. *Cruzan v. Director,* Missouri Dept. of Health (1990) 497 U.S. 261 (Cruzan).

CHAPTER THREE

Facts and Statistics

In Chapter 1, I discussed the ways you can make your treatment choices known to physicians. Actually, it is a bit more complicated than that.

What if I were to tell you that chemotherapy had a 10% chance of successfully treating your cancer? Would you want to try it? What if I told you the chemotherapy had a 90% chance of *not* being able to treat your cancer? Would you want to try it? You can see that I am giving you identical predictions. As it turns out, patients respond differently to these presentations of probabilities, one framed positively, the other framed negatively. They are more likely to accept a treatment if the choice is framed in terms of the probability of living rather than in terms of the probability of dying—even though the odds of predicted success are identical.[1,2,3]

When it comes to making tough decisions though, this is the easy part—a simple yes or no to two alternatives. What happens in practice is even *more* complicated. Patients suffering from a serious illness, along with their loved ones, often have to contend with a much greater variety of choices and probabilities, made no easier by the emotional burden of having to make the choices urgently, when the disease is harrowing and life-threatening. The physician may present the treatment alternatives not only in terms of probabilities of benefits but also the probabilities and timing of a variety of unwanted side effects, including death.

Consider again the patient with cancer, like Amelia Briggs, who is presented with alternative treatment choices, specifically surgery or radiation therapy. Surgery may have a higher probability of immediate death but a lower probability of death over time. Conversely, radiation could be expected to have a lower probability of short-term death but might have a higher probability of death in the long run. Which would *you* prefer?

Consider also that each intervention is associated with different side effects, the pains and discomforts of postsurgical convalescence versus the longer-term debilitation of high-dose radiation, including fatigue, nausea, skin rash, and loss of appetite. As the disease progresses, you may be confronted with similarly complicated treatment decisions again and again, each time unwittingly viewing the decisions through the distorting lens of positive and negative framing.

Not surprisingly, studies show that patients, as they contend with shifting medical circumstances, make treatment choices that seem to be rationally inconsistent, even contradictory. And, as time passes and the disease progresses, they (shocking!) sometimes change their minds.[3,4,5,6]

Even this simple observation, that patients are distracted from rational choice by the influence of framing, gets complicated the more one explores the phenomenon. In our own research, we confirmed that people were more likely to elect a treatment, such as surgery for a terminal liver disease, if it was presented in a positive frame. Looking beyond the individual, we also found that people were more likely to accept having their "father" give up an ICU bed to another patient if they were told the chances of his surviving were 90% on the general medical floor than if they were told his chances of dying were 10%. Therefore, framing influenced choices they would make for loved ones as well as for themselves. But when they were asked to make the same decision for a stranger ("Mr. Williams"), positive or negative framing had no effect. The choices of whether to give up the ICU bed were the same no matter how they were framed.[8]

In other words, it seems we can be much more rational about facts and statistics when we are asked to decide for strangers than for ourselves or for our loved ones. How many times do we read in the newspapers about tragic situations in which family members insist on medical treatments that "make no sense"? "How could they *do* that?" we wonder from our privileged distance.

Results of studies like these have important implications in the search for answers to the question: What should we do now? For one thing, they challenge our idealistic views of the sanctity of patient autonomy and informed consent. If human beings are not always rational in the way they process probabilities, how can we be sure that informed consent really represents informed *choice*?[7]

Moreover, you don't really have unlimited choices. You only get to choose those options presented by your physicians. And although patients today increasingly seek treatment information outside the doctor–patient encounter, most notably from the Internet (which I call the "misinformation highway" because so many sites are misleading), they, and you, still face another limitation: you can *refuse* any treatment; you cannot *demand* any treatment.

It gets even more interesting. Quite by accident, I happened upon another discovery about the influence of facts and statistics on patient choice. The patients in this case were actually healthcare professionals who were anxious about contracting AIDS. I was asked to lecture to them about their ethical duties in caring for patients who were positive for HIV. This was only a few years after the discovery of the virus, before the many new and effective Highly Active Anti-Retroviral treatments (HAART) and protease inhibitors became available. AIDS, although still ultimately fatal, is now viewed as a chronic illness. In those days, however, the average survival after detecting the infection was only 10 years. Surgeons were refusing to operate on patients with HIV, physicians and nurses were dreading the consequences of needle-stick injuries, and the media were full of debates about the wisdom and ethical obligations of providing emergency resuscitation on strangers.

Before a large roomful of doctors and nurses, I foolishly tried to show how "irrationally" we were behaving. After all, I chided them, we all had cared for patients with hepatitis B for many years before an effective protective vaccine existed. Simple calculations showed that the probability of death from accidental exposure to HIV was no worse than was the probability of death from accidental exposure to hepatitis B.

"Do the math," I said, referring to the law of joint probabilities. (Hold on, don't cringe or throw the book across the room—it's really very simple math. For example, to calculate joint probabilities—namely, the probability of coming up with heads both times when you flip two coins—you multiply the probabilities of coming up with heads for each coin flip. Because you have a 50% chance of getting heads with one coin and a 50%

chance of getting heads with the other coin, you simply multiply 50% times 50%, which is 25%. It is also easy to see as fractions: if you took one-half of something and then took one-half of that half, what you would be left with at the end is one-fourth. If you repeat this again and again—in other words, trying to flip three heads in a row or four heads in a row, and so forth—you can see that the probability of achieving this gets smaller and smaller. Which you already knew, of course. Now you know it better.)

I led the audience through the calculations for HIV and hepatitis B. The risk of contracting hepatitis B infection following accidental exposure was known by empirical observation to be high—in the range of 25%—because the virus is densely populous in the circulating blood. If we conservatively assume from the published literature that about 5% of those infected with hepatitis B die, either from fulminant or chronic progressive disease, then we multiply 25% (the risk of infection following exposure) times 5% (the risk of dying after infection) to arrive at a final risk of dying: about 1%. By contrast, the risk of HIV infection following accidental exposure was much lower—by then we knew it was no greater than 1%—because the circulating virus is more sparse. Multiply the 1% risk of contracting HIV infection following accidental exposure times the 100% risk of dying with the infection to arrive at a final risk of dying: again, about 1%.

Why then are we, who fearlessly cared for patients with hepatitis B, now so fearful of caring for patients with HIV, even *refusing* to care for them? Aren't we just sharing in society's hysteria, much of which was fanned by prejudice and ignorance against gay people and drug users?

At that moment, a nurse piped up: "Yes, but the problem is, once you get HIV infection you *know* you're going to die!"

What a remarkable—and for me, standing there lecturing the audience, deflating—concept. Even though any rational person could see that the odds of dying were the same, any fool could see that the certainty of death might be so undesirable that it might account for the greater concern about HIV than about hepatitis B. At that moment, this brave but anxious nurse made me realize we have to go beyond facts and statistics to empathy and the imagination.

The evidence is all around us, of course. Even though the risk of dying in an airplane is a minute fraction of the risk of dying in an automobile, people enter the solidly grounded vehicle every day without giving a thought to the risk of dying. Meanwhile, many people are so terrified of flying that they refuse to go up in the air. Why? Because, if something goes wrong up there in the air, it's a long way down. *You know you're going to die.*

One can also exercise one's imagination and realize that the experience leading to death is different. Fatal car crashes are instantaneous experiences. A drunk driver comes out of nowhere, swerves across the road, and hits you head on. You're alive one instant, dead the next. Over and done with. By contrast, one can imagine the prolonged despair of someone trapped in a falling airplane. In the same way, one can also imagine how agonizing it is to live for any length of time with a disease, knowing the outcome is inevitably fatal. What is true of HIV infection is also true of that most dreaded disease, cancer, whose ominous outcome is experienced as a daily burden, even to so-called "cancer survivors."

Is it so irrational then to consider and incorporate into our calculations the kinds of fears experienced by most, if not all, human beings?

All this got me to thinking. What really accounts for the difference in fear associated with accidental exposure to HIV and hepatitis B? Was it related to the stigma of HIV (which is what I thought at the beginning of my lecture) or to the inescapable risk of dying, the 100% mortality at the end, despite the initially small odds (which is what I thought at the end of my lecture)? I persuaded colleagues to help me answer this question. We designed a survey and gave it out to different groups of undergraduate students.[8] Here is the scenario in one questionnaire:

You have been shipwrecked on the shore of a tropical country. The only passage to safety is by one of two routes, both of which expose you to insects of varying population intensity and lethality. Route A sends you through a valley where your likelihood of being stung is 25%. The chance of dying if you are stung is 5%. Route B sends you through a valley in which the insects are sparser but more lethal. Through this route you have a 1% chance of being stung, but if you are stung you are 100% certain to die. Which route would you choose?

As you can see, we tested their response to the relative risks of dying in a scenario that mimicked the risks of hepatitis B and HIV, but excluded any mention of the diseases, hence any suggestion of stigma. In the second questionnaire, we presented the same contrasting odds, but this time we referred explicitly to accidental needle-stick exposure to hepatitis B versus HIV.

The idea was to see what influence on choice the various sequences of statistical risks played without any sense of stigma, in contrast with what influence on choice the same statistical risks played, this time associated with a stigmatized disease AIDS. We discovered that, indeed, even though the overall risks were the same, most students chose Route A and avoided Route B with its 100% certainty of dying. Surprisingly, it made no difference whether the risks were presented in terms of insects or diseases. Therefore, the "stigma" of AIDS did not materially affect their choices. So much for my suspicion that "AIDS hysteria" was the major factor in people's fears of HIV infection. It was—just as the nurse said—"*You know you're going to die!*"

And, like Woody Allen, people just don't want to be there when it happens.

FACTS, STATISTICS AND THE MEDIA

Before I leave this chapter, I would like to present another important feature of facts and statistics. Most of us rely on mainstream journalism to provide the kind of information that allows us to draw informed conclusions about the latest medical headlines. Unfortunately, most journalists do not understand, much less present, the information under the headlines objectively and accurately. This is particularly glaring when facts and statistics are involved. Almost invariably, they fail to make the important distinction between "relative risk reduction" and "absolute risk reduction" when reporting the results of a new "miracle drug." (Once again, don't cringe. The math is simple and straightforward.)

You might read a headline declaring that Drug A is "Twice as Effective!" as Drug B in reducing mortality in cancer. What is rarely reported in the accompanying story are the important details that distinguish between the relative risk reduction and absolute risk reduction of death. For example, if only 40 out of 100 patients treated with Drug A died of cancer while 80 out of 100 patients treated with Drug B died of cancer, you would be impressed and agree with headlines that declare that Drug A is "Twice as Effective!" Indeed, *relative* to Drug B, Drug A seemed to reduce the risk of death in twice as many patients. Also, you would be impressed with the *absolute* reduction of the risk of death because 40 (40%) more patients out of 100 were spared death from cancer with Drug A than with Drug B. Drug A also seemed to be pretty effective as a cancer treatment because it seemed to work in 80 out of 100 patients. In other words, you needed to treat only 10 patients to save 8, while Drug B saved only 4.

But what if only 2 patients with cancer out of 100 treated with Drug A survived, and only 1 patient with cancer out of 100 treated with Drug B survived? Once again, because *relative* to Drug B, twice as many patients treated with Drug A survived, the headline proclaiming that Drug A was "Twice as Effective!" in preventing death would still seem to be true. But, clearly, you would be much less impressed. You wouldn't have to do any sophisticated statistical tests to determine whether the difference was "significant" because the *absolute* difference was only 1% (1 of 100 patients). That's what you really want to know, the absolute risk reduction— the essential information missing from most news reports. Note also the large number of patients (100) who needed to be treated by Drug A (and subjected to possible side effects) to prevent the additional death that occurred with Drug B. You would have to treat 50 patients with Drug A to save 1 patient's life, and 100 patients with Drug B to save 1 patient's life. Clearly, neither of these drugs is very effective.

We've looked at the *intended benefits* of a drug—namely, its ability to reduce the risk of dying of cancer. The same calculations hold for the opposite—namely, the *unintended risks* of side effects caused by the drug. Again we have to make a distinction, this time between relative risk and absolute risk. This distinction was completely lost in the media swirl when the pharmaceutical company Merck admitted that serious thrombotic events (including heart attack and stroke) were associated with its new selective cyclooxygenase (COX-2) inhibitor Vioxx®. Although the shrill headlines announcing the relative risks certainly were scary (more than twice the risk!), the absolute risk was not presented for public consideration. The manufacturer simply removed the drug from the market.

Merck was conducting a 3-year randomized controlled trial involving 2,600 patients to determine whether treatment with Vioxx, a drug with promising preliminary data as a cancer preventive, would prevent the recurrence of cancerous polyps in patients with a history of colorectal polyps. Halfway through the trial, the researchers discovered that heart attacks or strokes occurred in approximately 3 per 400 patient years in those taking the placebo and in 6 per 400 patient years in those taking Vioxx.[9]

Thus, it is true that twice as many adverse events occurred in the patients who took Vioxx as in the patients who took the placebo. That was the relative risk. But note how the perspective changes when one looks at the absolute risk: three additional events per 400 patient years, a far less scary increase of less than 1%. Looked at from even another perspective, 396 patients per year at high risk for colon cancer, who might have been benefiting from the drug, experienced no adverse event. Was the potential benefit of escaping cancer worth the risk? Would the swift death from a heart attack be preferable to a lingering death from cancer? Some patients might think so. But Merck executives did not let them decide for themselves. Rather, the drug executives sent nervous, furtive e-mails back and forth as they debated what to do about the unsettling data. As anyone knows, e-mails are like postcards, because they eventually are discoverable; when the press got hold of them, a scandal erupted and the drug was pulled.

Merck had tried to keep all their discussions and e-mail exchanges secret to avoid what may become astronomically costly lawsuits. (About 20 million patients received Vioxx prescriptions, and Merck now faces thousands of lawsuits from plaintiffs who contend that the drug caused heart attacks and strokes.) Ironically, it's not the facts and statistics that are propelling the lawsuits so much as the discovery of e-mails and other evidence of withholding information and deception. We've heard that before: *It's not the crime but the cover-up.* Meanwhile, no attention is being paid to the vastly larger group of participants who were not harmed. These are patients at risk of developing colon cancer. Are their interests being served?

A similar study of a similar COX-2 inhibitor, Celebrex, also made the headlines (more than three times the risks of heart attacks, strokes, and death!) Once again, the absolute differences were less impressive than the relative differences. Here are the randomized controlled data: 6 cardiac events occurred in approximately 600 patients given a placebo, 15 cardiac events in approximately 600 patients given the low-dose medication, and 20 cardiac events in approximately 600 patients given the high-dose medication.[10]

Therefore, the increase in absolute risk to patients taking the drug was in the range of only 2% to 3%. Meanwhile, the relative risks showed that twice as many patients in the placebo group developed colorectal cancer and twice as many patients on the drug experienced "cardiovascular events" ("Twice the benefit!" "Twice the risk!"). Once again, however, in absolute terms, both the benefit and risk were small (less than 1%). Clearly, not a great drug.

But is the benefit worth the risk? Two commentators in the *New England Journal of Medicine* decided it was not.[11] In reaching their judgment, however, they gave colorectal cancer and cardiovascular events "equal weight." Please do not think I am despairing over these indentations in the drug companies' fortunes. Their drugs are expensive, and their benefits may be achievable more cheaply by simple aspirin and nonsteroidal anti-inflammatory drugs (NSAIDS). What I despair at is the exclusion of an enlightened patient from these decisions.

Indeed, more recent extensive data compiled for the U.S. Preventive Services Task Force show that all three categories of drugs (aspirin, NSAIDS, and COX-2 inhibitors) seem to be effective at reducing the incidence of colonic adenoma and colorectal cancer.[12,13,14] The problem? An increase in cardiovascular "events," like stroke and heart attacks and gastrointestinal "harms" like peptic ulcers and bleeding. The enlightened patient might note, of course, that these "events" and "harms," as undesirable as they are, did not lead to increased mortality. Which leads to the question: Would patients at high risk for cancer who are being denied access to a promising cancer preventive give equal weight to these conditions in their risk/benefit analysis? For example, is dying from cancer no different from dying of a heart attack? As one layperson complained, "Did the heart risk really outweigh the possible benefit, even in cancer patients or people at high risk? The answer is still not entirely clear."[15] Why? Because comparing different subjective experiences among different patients does not lend itself well to statistical analysis.

We are left with other questions whose answers are not clear. Could an informed press, able to explain the data more clearly, have prevented the Vioxx fiasco? Will drug companies like Merck ever trust the press to join them in the more difficult and less sensational enterprise of providing, rather than hiding, these data? Wouldn't it be great if an informed public were let in on these decisions? In short, is there a place for the enlightened patient in this age of "miracles"?

REFERENCES

1. McNeil, BJ, Pauker SG, Sox HC, Tversky A. On the elicitation of preferences for alternative therapies. *New England Journal of Medicine* (1982) 306:1259–62.

2. Wilson DK, Kaplan RM, Schneiderman LJ. Framing of decisions and selections of alternatives in health care. *Social Behavior* (1987) 2:51–9.

3. Schneiderman LJ, Pearlman RA, Kaplan RM, Anderson JP, Rosenberg EM. Relationship of general advance directive instructions to specific life-sustaining treatment preferences in patients with serious illness. *Archives of Internal Medicine* (1992) 152:2114–22.

4. Schneiderman LJ, Kronick R, Kaplan RM, Anderson JP, Langer RD. Effects of offering advance directives on medical treatments and costs: a prospective study. *Annals of Internal Medicine* (1992) 1176:599–606.

5. Boyd NF, Sutherland HJ, Heasman KZ, Tritchler DL, Cummings BJ. Whose utilities for decision analysis? *Medical Decision Making* (1990) 10:58–67.

6. Christensen-Szalanski JJ. Discount functions and the measurement of patients' values: women's decisions during childbirth. *Medical Decision Making* (1984) 4:47–58.

7. Teversky A, Kahneman D. The framing of decisions and the psychology of choice. *Science* (1981) 211:453–8.

8. Schneiderman LJ, Kaplan RM. Fear of dying and HIV infection vs Hepatitis B infection. *Am J Public Health* (1992) 82:584–586.

9. Immediate withdrawal of Rofecoxib (Vioxx/Vioxxacute) report of *The Committee on Safety of Medicines.* infoAmhra.gsi.gov.uk

10. Harris G. Drug Trial Finds Big Health Risks in 2nd Painkiller. *The New York Times.* December 18, 2004.

11. Pasty BM, Potter JD. Risks and benefits of celecoxib to prevent recurrent adenomas. *New England Journal of Medicine* (2006) 355: 950–2.

12. *U.S. Preventive Services Task Force.* Routine aspirin or nonsteroidal anti-inflammatory drugs for the primary prevention of colorectal cancer: U.S. Preventive Services Task Force recommendation statement. *Annals of Internal Medicine* (2007) 146:361–4.

13. Dube C, Rostom A, Lewin G, et al. The use of aspirin for primary prevention of colorectal cancer: a systematic review prepared for the U.S. Preventive Services Task Force. *Annals of Internal Medicine* (2007) 146:365–75.

14. Rostom A, Dube C, Lewin G, et al. Nonsteroidal anti-inflammatory drugs and cyclooxygenase-2 inhibitors for primary prevention of colorectal cancer: a systematic review prepared for the U.S. Preventive Services Task Force. *Annals of Internal Medicine* (2007) 146:376–89.

15. Grady D. When Hopes For a Drug Are Dashed, What Then? *The New York Times.* Tuesday, September 5, 2006. D5.

CHAPTER FOUR

Empathy and Imagination

Now, let's take a break from facts and statistics and see whether there is even more we can learn from exercising our empathy and imagination.

Early in my medical career, while trying to persuade Cathy Meadows (not her real name), an adolescent patient with diabetes, to attend more carefully to her diet and insulin, I heard my voice echo in a strange chamber of my memory. Not the medical lecture hall with its erudite revelations of glucose and lipid metabolism, hyperglycemic pathologies, and insulin mechanisms of action, but rather the stunted, plaintive, haunted world of J. D. Salinger. Remember, I was a literature major in college.

Before I go further, I must point out that as rapturously complex as diabetes mellitus is to the research scientist, the options available to the medical practitioner for treating this teenager were brutally simple: diet and insulin.

The concepts and instructions I imparted were well within her comprehension. Yet it was impossible for me to "manage" her disease. Cathy was the only one who could do so, a task she sullenly avoided even as her eyes, under her matted hair, which she periodically shook into new disorders, avoided mine. As a result, this emotionally windswept young woman was in and out of life-threatening hypoglycemia and diabetic coma and, of course, in and out of the hospital.

Her future, I kept trying to remind her, grew dimmer with each lapse—which, I added encouragingly, could be avoided by the simplest of measures: diet and insulin. I heard myself endlessly repeating: "Do you understand me? Tell me what you are thinking. Why are you doing these things to yourself?"

And then the source of the echo came to me: the scene in *The Catcher in the Rye* when Holden Caulfield's English teacher, in the most kind, persistent way tries to understand why his young student is failing.[1]

"Tell the truth, boy," his teacher implores.

But the teenager is not about to lay truth across the yawning chasm between him and this old man. Rather, he regards his excruciatingly well-intentioned mentor from another world entirely:

> "Well, you can see he felt pretty lousy about flunking me. So I shot the bull for a while. I told him I was a real moron, and all that stuff. I told him how I would have done exactly the same thing if I'd been in his place, and how most people didn't appreciate how tough it is being a teacher. That kind of stuff. The old bull."

Meanwhile the dedicated teacher pursues the issue with all his heart. "How do you *feel* about all of this boy? I would be very interested to know. Very interested."

Holden Caulfield never responds to the teacher's entreaties. He barely tolerates the sight of that repellent alien object—an old man. ("I sort of wish he'd cover up his bumpy chest. It wasn't such a beautiful view.") Nor does he even bother to explain his silence. ("I didn't feel like going into the whole thing with him. He wouldn't have understood it anyway. It wasn't up his alley at all.")

And so, as I sat before this young woman whose eyes listed one way, then another, barely tolerating the sight of me, I realized that I too was experiencing that aching frustration that has no parallel—the adolescent embarked on willful self-destruction. It didn't matter that it was her very life we were talking about. No amount of good will on my part could overcome her stubborn self-imposed deafness to my entreaties. Indeed, nothing could compensate for the crime I had committed, that pre-empted everything else in her hierarchy of values: I was one of *them*—an *un*-teenager. "Like *to*tally for*get* it!" How could *any*thing I say be of the *slight*est interest to her? Indeed, as far as she was concerned, having forfeited my rights by growing old (I was then in my thirties), I was lucky she was deigning to grant me even that much of her time. And yet, though I could do nothing about it, I persuaded myself I could at least *feel* how she felt, fortified by the imagination of J. D. Salinger.

It was not my scientific training or even my medical training that helped me make this emotional connection. Rather it was the experience of literary fiction. But notice I said "imagination." Salinger's skill at imagining the fictional monologue of an alienated teenager helped me imagine that I had achieved a state of shared feeling with the alienated teenager in front of me. Was this empathy or was it self-delusion? Did it help me heal the young woman? Not really. Cathy continued her difficult ways. In time we both moved on and I lost track of her.

So then, what good is empathy? Why seek it? One physician says it will help fellow physicians overcome "[i]solation, long hours of service, chronic lack of sleep, sadness at prolonged human tragedies, and depression at futile and often incomprehensible therapeutic maneuvers. . . . "[2] But, if that's the only benefit of empathy, then wouldn't kind companionship, soothing drugs, longer hours of sleep, and more frequent vacations do as well?

Shouldn't we expect more? Shouldn't empathy make us better physicians?

The closer we get to the feelings of our patients, goes the argument, the better we can understand them. The better we understand them, the closer we come to discovering the true state of affairs, and the more likely we will be able to diagnose and treat correctly. This is how novels, stories, and other works of art are supposed to help us. As a physician and writer, I have to confess: I both believe and doubt this.

More recently, while taking an interval history from Joe Hoover (not his real name), a 70-year-old man with progressive congestive heart failure whom I briefly described in the Introduction, I did what every good clinician does: I tried to get things down in precise numbers. I sought exact quantities; not only weight, pulse, blood pressure, and vital lung capacity, but also measures of activity: How many blocks could he walk; how many stairs could he climb? I inserted these questions as deftly as I could into his charming, meandering discourse on life's occasions.

A brief passage of words almost slipped by me; indeed I do not recall how long it took me to notice them after they were uttered.

Something about apricots. Every year at this time, Joe was murmuring, he likes to putter in his garden. Lately, he could no longer capture the apricots at the very top of the trees . . . and that's when the words appeared, mildly rueful, with a self-effacing cough and smile—"The story of my life." He paused, and it was the pause that allowed me to spot the words in the underbrush of all the others, made me realize how central was this aside. The story of his life—and the most important measure of his deteriorating health—was not the stairs he could no longer climb, nor the blocks he could no longer walk. It was the fruits at the tops of trees this modern-day Tantalus could no longer reach. My ballpoint pen circled in a holding pattern over my notes. Where among my numbers could I put this remark, this most revealing utterance, this line of poetry, this statement both specific and profound that went utterly to the heart of Joe Hoover's existence? I finally honored it with a line all its own to ensure it would not be overlooked. *Patient states: "I can no longer reach the apricots at the tops of the trees. The story of my life."*

It was my bow to Literature. Indeed, this stirring of empathy diverted me to ask more about his garden, his trees, his apricots. I learned that he produced them by the bushel. "What do you do with them all?" I asked. Joe's eyes lit up proudly. "Make pies for my friends," he said. "I used to make dozens of pies." Immediately, however, I felt the impatient flick of Medicine's riding crop, and resumed collecting my numbers—how else would I know whether my treatments were helping him? "And how many pies can you make now?" I heard myself babble.

I must confess to you now that I myself have committed fiction. My stories often begin to germinate when something unsettling occurs—some word, some gesture, some image that remains net-tlesome and restless long after the event. An awkward silence, a clumsy half-ashamed and hastily retracted complaint, eyes that avoided mine—disturbing signs that I missed something, a meaning, a connection, a vital, now irretrievable secret. Whenever this happens, naturally I try to figure out what went wrong. But if I fail to correct my oversight or make up for my failure, I still have my imagination. My imagination is wonderfully tolerant. It allows me to retract and remake history by infusing into the present my own memories from the past. How did that person feel when this happened? How is that feeling similar to feelings I have had? What can I do to make up for what happened? What would I have wanted for myself? This process, we are told, is empathy. It is also the workings of the literary imagination. One, we are told, brings us closer to the truth. The other is conspicuously false. What is one to believe?

Like many writers, I keep a notebook in which I write down snatches of overheard conversations; descriptions of gestures, events, words, and phrases I impulsively fall in love with, moments I observe in the everyday life around me.

When I began to do this many years ago I assumed that the notebooks would provide me with a sumptuous smorgasbord for my writing. But I rarely make use of them. Except for an odd note here and there, these observations hardly ever coincide with what I'm making up at the moment. It should have been self-evident, but it wasn't to me: Fiction is not reality. A work of fiction has its own impulse, its own momentum, its own boundaries. In writing my stories I mix things together, pounding and stretching, even twisting off and throwing away parts that don't fit some personal esthetic command.

Fiction, that is, the literary imagination, is not about what happened, but about a whole cosmos of happenings—what might have happened, or could have happened, or, if you delve into the psyche of the author, what should have happened. Fiction, unlike science, cannot be validated by experimental confirmation. Like any art form, fiction is revered only if it is unique, something no other artist created, whereas the whole point of science is to discover something common, something other scientists would inevitably discover. Mozart did not have to race against other composers to be the first to produce his Requiem. He raced against death. Without him the work would never exist. But as we well know, Watson and Crick were in a hell-bent race to be first to get credit for discovering what others were on the verge of also discovering and ended up merely confirming—the fundamental structure and function of genetic DNA.

I point out these differences because those of us in medicine are immersed in the scientific method of validation. Empathy, however, can never be validated by formal objective external processes. (Yet—how frustrating—we know there's a *there* there, the counterpart to objective reality, the patient's true emotional state.) Rather, it shares a property of the literary imagination in that it can only be felt. Therefore, because its validation at best arrives through internal subjective emotional processes, it will remain eternally elusive.

In my own life I am very aware of this duality. When it comes to reporting my medical or scientific observations, I curb my imagination. I would never dare fudge data in the slightest. What would be the point? Without the confirmation by other researchers, they would not be believed, and therefore would not exist. But when I set a short story down on paper, I give my imagination free rein to create a fictional world. I strive to make you, the reader, believe. I can look to no one else for confirmation. I have to persuade you myself.

As I mentioned in the Introduction, I teach an elective course for medical students called "The Good Doctor, The Literature and Medicine of Anton Chekhov (and Others)." In weekly seminars, we read and discuss some of the short stories and a play or two of this acknowledged master, who surveyed the great range of life from the poorest peasant to the wealthiest landowner, from the spiritually naive or crude or retarded to the most sophisticated, artistically cultivated, and exquisitely educated. Especially endearing to me is that Chekhov effaced his own personality so completely and imagined his characters so successfully that a reader who did not know would never guess he was a physician. I try to use this physician–writer as a model for the students. Doctors have already written plenty of stories revealing what it is like to be a doctor—nowadays, I tell them, it's all the rage. Let's not be so narcissistic. Let's try empathy. And the task I set them is this: Imagine what it is like to be anything but a doctor. Imagine what it is like to be a patient, a close friend, a lover, a family member, because *that* is the world you must understand. And so for their final paper, I require them to write a short story with a nonmedical narrator and point of view. In short, I am seeking through literature to be empathic.

But as I already warned you, in my fiction, everything has been made up. Real life has been distorted. A story seeks its own reality, its own entirety, out of parts manufactured by twisting and squeezing elements of both recognizable reality and idiosyncratic fantasy (or if not fantasy, possibly unconsciously remembered—although surely distorted—reality) into some amalgam of all these. What you and I would call "the truth" is nothing like that. Even J. D. Salinger, the inspiration for my empathy for Cathy, the adolescent diabetic, would say the same thing, I'm sure.

What then is the connection between literature and empathy? Is any story of mine really an empathic reaching to the truth? Or am I committing the very opposite act, projecting my limited imagination and thereby creating utter falsehood? What is it we all do, really, whether we call ourselves writers (and admit our falsehood) or call ourselves empathic physicians (and overlook our arrogant presumption)?

Because I aspire to both roles, I admit I am culpable on both these charges. And yet, may I not claim—and is it not possible—that the search for a fictional truth is an exploration into deeper universal realities? Though specific details, grounded in reality, are essential to bringing the fictional character to life, any good writer will tell you that if a story somehow fails to connect with the reader or communicate with any vividness or power—in other words, if the story fails to move the reader—it is not a defense for the author to claim "But that's the way it really happened." In fiction, reality has no standing.

Shakespeare's unnatural speech issues forth from costumed actors posturing on a wooden stage, who fall down pretending to be dead, then spring up in time to bow before a curtain—that's the reality. Yet Shakespeare's art, despite these obstacles, far beyond the capacity of these obstacles to obstruct with reality its blatant, magnificent falsity, that *art* has seized human beings for centuries as truthfully revealing their highest and lowest impulses and possibilities. Shakespeare's imagination radiates the full range, not merely what it is to be Hamlet or Juliet or Iago or Lady Macbeth or Lear, but what it is to be *human,* like Hamlet *and*

Juliet *and* Iago *and* Lady Macbeth *and* Lear. And so on. And so on.[3]

The truth is, great art does move us more powerfully toward this discovery than the most scrupulous reality.

REFERENCES

1. Salinger, J. D. *The Catcher in the Rye.* Boston: Little Brown, 1951: 12–13.
2. Spiro H. What is empathy and can it be taught? *Annals of Internal Medicine* (1992) 116: 843–46.
3. Bloom H. *Shakespeare: The Invention of the Human.* New York: Riverhead Books, 1998.

CHAPTER FIVE

Ancient Myth and Modern Medicine: What Can We Learn From the Past?

Back in grade school, when I came upon *Bulfinch's Mythology*,[1] I never dreamed it would someday help me practice medicine. At the time all that mattered was how wonderful they were, the adventures of all those old Greek gods. I read the stories again and again, at an innocent age, so innocent I—like the ancient Greeks themselves[2]—believed they all were true (which may have accounted for their permanent impression on me). One of my favorite memories is the tale of Baucis and Philemon. How strange that this ancient myth could be of use to a modern physician. Here it is, as recorded in *Bulfinch's Mythology*:

> **On a certain hill in Phrygia stands a linden tree and an oak, enclosed by a low wall. Not far from the spot is a marsh, formerly good habitable land, but now indented with pools, the resort of fen-birds and cormorants. Once**

on a time Jupiter, in human shape, visited this country, and with him his son Mercury (he of the caduceus), without his wings. They presented themselves, as weary travelers, at many a door, seeking rest and shelter, but found all closed, for it was late, and the inhospitable inhabitants would not rouse themselves to open for their reception. At last a humble mansion received them, a small thatched cottage, where Baucis, a pious old dame, and her husband Philemon, united when young, had grown old together. Not ashamed of their poverty, they made it endurable by moderate desires and kind dispositions. One need not look there for master or for servant; they two were the whole household, master and servant alike. When the two heavenly guests crossed the humble threshold, and bowed their heads to pass under the low door, the old man placed a seat, on which Baucis, bustling and attentive, spread a cloth, and begged them to sit down. Then she raked out the coals from the ashes, and kindled up a fire, fed it with leaves and dry bark, and with her scanty breath blew it into a flame. She brought out of a corner split sticks and dry branches, broke them up, and placed them under the small kettle. Her husband collected some pot-herbs in the garden, and she shred them from the stalks, and prepared them the pot. He reached down with a forked stick a flitch of bacon hanging in the chimney, cut a small piece, and put it in the pot to boil with the herbs, setting away the rest for another time. A beechen bowl was filled with warm water, that their guests might wash. While all was doing they beguiled the time with conversation.

On the bench designed for the guests was laid a cushion stuffed with sea-weed; and a cloth, only produced on great occasions, but ancient and coarse enough, was spread over that. The old lady, with her apron on, with trembling hands set the table. One leg was shorter than the rest, but a piece of slate put under restored the level. When fixed, she rubbed the table down with some sweet-smelling herbs. Upon it she set some of chaste Minerva's olives, some cornel berries preserved in vinegar, and added radishes and cheese, with eggs lightly cooked in the ashes. All were served in earthen dishes, and an earthenware pitcher, with wooden cups, stood beside them. When all was ready, the stew, smoking hot, was set on the table. Some wine, not of the oldest, was added; and for dessert, apples and wild honey; and over and above all, friendly faces, and simple but hearty welcome.

Now while the repast proceeded, the old folks were astonished to see that the wine, as fast as it was poured out, renewed itself in the pitcher, of its own accord. Struck with terror, Baucis and Philemon recognized their heavenly guests, fell on their knees, and with clasped hands implored forgiveness for their poor entertainment. There was an old goose, which they kept as the guardian of their humble cottage; and they bethought them to make this a sacrifice in honor of their guests. But the goose, too nimble, with the aid of feet and wings, for the old folks, eluded their pursuit, and at last took shelter between the gods themselves. They forbade it to be slain; and spoke in these words: "We are gods. This inhospitable village shall pay the penalty of its impiety; you alone shall go free from the chastisement. Quit your house, and come with us to the top of yonder hill." They hastened to obey, and, staff in hand, laboured up the steep ascent. They had reached to within an arrow's flight of the top, when, turning their eyes below, they beheld all the country sunk in a lake, only their own house left standing. While they gazed with wonder at the sight, and lamented the fate of their neighbors, that old house of theirs was changed into a temple. Columns took the place of the corner posts, the thatch grew yellow and appeared a gilded roof, the floors became marble, the doors were enriched with carving and ornaments of gold. Then spoke Jupiter in benignant accents: "Excellent old man, and woman worthy of such a husband, speak, tell us our wishes; what favour have you to ask of us?" Philemon took counsel with Baucis a few moments; then declared to the gods their united wish. "We ask to be priests and guardians of this your temple; and since here we have passed our lives in love and concord, we wish that one and the same hour may take us both from life, that I may not live to see her grave, nor be laid in my own by her." Their prayer was granted. They were the keepers of the temple as long as they lived. When grown very old, as they stood one day before the steps of the sacred edifice, and were telling the story of the place, Baucis saw Philemon begin to put forth leaves, and old Philemon saw Baucis changing in like manner. And now a leafy crown had grown over their heads, while exchanging parting words, as long as they could speak. "Farewell, dear spouse," they said, together, and at the same moment the bark closed over their mouths. The Tyanean shepherd still

**shows the two trees, standing side by side, made out of the
two good old people.**

Over the years I've had many occasions to meditate on this myth
while caring for my elderly patients. Surprising, because it is just a
story, after all. As an evidence-based, modern-day physician, I know
I am supposed to be skeptical of anecdotal evidence. Many of the
miracles of modern medicine have been achieved by overthrowing
the myths of the past and replacing them with dogged empiricism.
Okay, admittedly medicine is infiltrated with moral questions, and
the ancient Greeks did have some interesting moral answers back
when life was simple. But what have they done for us lately? What
can they teach us about organ transplantation, gene therapy, nu-
clear transfer, embryonic stem cells, artificial insemination, surrogate motherhood, DNAR orders, prolongation of vegetative
existence, allocation of ICU beds? Not only medicine but life itself
has become so much more complicated. We live in a vast country,
derived from a plethora of cultures, sharing no common religion,
and constantly interacting with an even vaster more complex world.

For example, take the great classical art form: drama. Unlike
today's audience, which demands novelty and variety from the play-
wright, the ancient Greeks flocked to the ceremonies of drama to
experience the familiar. A single Oedipus plot served many plays,
and any number of playwrights, including the celebrated ones—
Sophocles, Euripides, Aeschylus, Aristophanes. What would compare in these more pluralistic and secular times? "George Washington and the Cherry Tree," dramatized by Arthur Miller, David
Mamet, Sam Shepard, August Wilson, Neil Simon? Obviously the
role of such legends in society—except as occasional sources for

fluffy musicals—has greatly diminished. Have they entirely lost their relevance?

I remember when the myth of Baucis and Philemon first entered my medical ruminations. I was seeing George and Carol Koh (not their real names). Both were in their seventies. However, fate had treated him far more kindly than her. Carol was definitely in the category of "looking older than her stated age"—frail, requiring help for her simplest everyday tasks, and utterly terrified at the thought of leaving the security of her home. George, on the other hand, was still physically vigorous, bouncy, cheerful, and extroverted. He had conceived the fanciful notion of traveling continuously around the world in whatever years were left to him. However, Carol was not up to it. I could see that their marriage vows of "for better or for worse" and "in sickness and in health" were being sorely tested. Although he applied the most devoted attentions to his wife, Mr. Koh chafed at the restrictions on his life. This only added guilt to Mrs. Koh's suffering.

I had come upon a terrible secret—the pain lurking for two people bound by love, made all the worse by love, in their unequal passage through life. Ahead lay the prospect of loneliness and vulnerability to fate. Then I remembered the wish that Baucis and Philemon had made to the gods: **" . . . [S]ince here we have passed our lives in love and concord, we wish that one and the same hour take us both from life, that I may not live to see her grave, nor be laid in my own by her."**

It struck me that the two mythological characters had asked not for health or beauty or riches or long life or any other miraculous gift the gods presumably were up to providing, but merely to be granted a simultaneous death. Since then I have discovered that this terrible secret—the desirability of timing one person's death to match another's—is no secret to the elderly.

My meditations continued when I cared for Bernard and Susan Lowry (not their real names). Now in their eighties, they had been discussing their future with me for all the nearly 20 years they had been in my care. At first, Bernard's health was more precarious. When they came to me he already had diabetes, high blood pressure, painful arthritis, a hernia, and symptomatic prostate trouble. Susan, on the other hand, was sharp-witted, socially active, energetic, intent that the two of them continue to "use it and not lose it"—definitely the more promising of the two. We frankly addressed their prospects under the not unreasonable assumption that Susan would be the caretaker and ultimate survivor, a calculation made all the more likely after Bernard developed atrial fibrillation, heart failure, and bilateral atherosclerotic obstruction of his femoral arteries, which required an aortic bypass procedure. Would Susan be able to care for Bernard, I wondered, and how would she get along when he was gone?

Astonishingly Bernard came through his surgery, experienced a revival in his spirits and physical ability, and even took up an exercise program of golf several times a week. Meanwhile Susan began to show the earliest signs of Progressive Supranuclear Palsy, a relentless neurological deterioration resembling Parkinson's disease—it was she whose life suddenly took a downward course. Her husband had to assist her with walking, and scurrying about as best he could to protect this willful—to the point of reckless—woman from crashing to the floor. When we managed to persuade her to use a wheelchair, it allowed him to push her around the retirement village. Although she could barely speak, at least she could listen to conversations he engaged in with other residents.

In the last year his career took a turn for the worse. He fell and fractured his spine. Despite medications, his various illnesses (including progressive heart failure) forced him to abandon his golf game and limit his walking to short distances. Despite all his own problems, Bernard's first question and the one with greatest feeling was: "How am I going to take care of her?"

It was clear that their long lives together were coming to an end, but who could have predicted this spiraling trajectory? Both agreed—and openly discussed—that if Susan died first, it would not be as bad as if Bernard died first. Where would she go? What would happen to her? Their children could not give her the total attention Bernard gave her. She would rather have died than go to a nursing home. Every utterance seemed to echo Baucis and Philemon: **"We wish that one and the same hour may take us both from life."**

I thought: What would the American Association of Retired Persons (AARP) say if they could hear her speak? They would clearly be alarmed. Susan met the suicide "warning signs" of the AARP's Public Policy Institute: social isolation and loneliness; a history of recent losses and intractable pain; change in status related to income, employment, and independence; and fear of institutionalization in a nursing home. Yet, what does the myth say? That a good and timely death no less than a good and timely life is a gift of the gods. Is it proof of society's advancement that our modern gods would not grant Baucis and Philemon their wish?

Passing on. This much-mocked euphemism for dying can also represent the obvious fact that when we die we pass on what we have possessed to those who follow us. Baucis and Philemon did not ask to join the immortal gods but rather "**to be priests and guardians of this your temple**." In other words, to remain on earth and be the temporary stewards of the symbols of their benedictions.

The elderly are no different from anyone else in wanting to enjoy their lives to the fullest. However, as described in Chapter 2, many dread outstaying their welcome, becoming a burden, leaving nothing but bitterness as their memorial.

My clinical experience and research, as well as the research of others, indicate that most elderly patients do not want to be kept alive with aggressive medical measures if, for example, they become permanently unconscious, and do not want life support treatments if it means living permanently attached to a ventilator or requiring artificial nutrition. At some point they want to pass on. They object to exhausting their life savings on these kinds of interventions not only from personal economic considerations but also from the desire to pass on to children and grandchildren property, acquisitions, memorabilia, monetary and other legacies—proofs of their existence.

It is a common experience that at some point almost every dying person accepts the inevitable. Unlike the young (and animals), who never imagine themselves growing old, much less dying, the elderly contemplate their deaths in considerable detail—this is evident by any survey that has been performed regarding their wishes for terminal care. I thought: How modest, simple, and rudimentary is the world of Baucis and Philemon. The threshold the two heavenly guests cross is "humble"; they eat out of "earthen" dishes and "wooden" cups on a cloth that is "ancient and coarse." The goose they attempt to catch and serve is old and their last. Even the rickety table needs the prosthetic assistance of a piece of slate. Every detail serves to underscore what today would be called their marginal socio-economic state. However, **"not ashamed of their poverty, they made it endurable by moderate desires and kind dispositions."**

One day, most of my time with Rosanne Paladio (not her real name) was spent trying to cheer her and help her figure out ways to pass the time. She admits to being old (in her late seventies) but not to being ill, except for dizzy spells, which prevent her from driving her car. Only miserably bored. Which she would not be, indeed she would have no complaints at all if only she could just *go* places—local museums, the library, art galleries, a few concerts and lectures, a few senior citizen and Sierra club activities. These simple capacities would be all she needed to improve those measures of health social researchers love to collect—activity level, quality of well-being, locus of control, sense of coherence, and so forth. However, this city, in which two hospitals are jostling to promote their heart-lung transplant programs, provides her no affordable way to get around. The public transportation and Dial-a-Ride systems are pathetically inadequate. Our governmental gods could grant her wish if it were for a heart-lung transplant. Medicare would pay the hundreds of thousands of dollars for the procedure, in addition to drugs, biopsies, specialists, and complex follow-up care. But the gods ordained no medical insurance that pays for taxicabs. In an age of technological splendor, Rosanne suffered from the simplest forms of deprivation which, as her physician, I tried to help make endurable by "moderate desires" (for conversation) and "kind (and frustrated) dispositions."

One day I noticed tears in the eyes of Susan Lowry, the elderly women patient who suffered from the Parkinson's-like disease. Her husband was describing their activities since I had last seen them. I interrupted to ask her how she felt. Haltingly, but with the force of despair, she said, "I feel life has betrayed me."

I could picture her life somewhat because I had made a house call to get an idea of where she lived and, in particular, to help the two of them identify and minimize injury hazards. As I wandered around her retirement complex, I could not help thinking again of Baucis and Philemon—exchanging parting words, putting forth leaves, metamorphosing into a linden tree and an oak—climaxing a story in which images of transforming nature abound. From the very beginning the story tells of time's passage and how it causes not only decay but replenishment. The setting is **"a marsh, normally good habitable land, but now indented with pools, the resort of fen birds and cormorants."** Wine is miraculously restored in the pitcher, and a flood engulfs the village and transforms their house into an opulent temple, echoing other replenishment myths—Jesus and the wine, Noah and the Ark, to name just two. Life ends, life renews, the story says.

In contrast there were no reassuring images of nature's renewal to comfort Susan Lowry. The retirement village was trimly landscaped with low maintenance shrubs bred to the perfection of artificial flowers. Rarely do they drop a leaf onto the tidy banks of redwood chips. The materials of her world consist of glabrous stucco, tile, wrought iron, and molded plastic furniture. The chlorinated pool was not the fertile resort of fen-birds and cormorants but only of the regulars who did their daily laps. Instead of a muddy path scattered with surprises, she had glaring swathes of concrete; instead of rocky hillsides, she had the comforts of elevators; instead of weather, she had air conditioning. The slightest hint of decay was hastily repaired and nothing intruded into the well-maintained blandness. Life for her was an unchanging schedule of card games she could not join, conversations she could only listen to, and exercise classes she could only watch. As senior citizens residencies go, it was considered one of the best.

We cannot know for certain, but the gods' appointment of Baucis and Philemon as **"keeper of the temple as long as they live"** suggests that the elderly played a vital, even powerful, role close to the central symbols of religious worship in classical Greek society. From our utilitarian perspective, we might wonder why they were given such a place of honor in a period of history that surely must have been dominated by want, hardship, and uncertainty, not to mention the requirements of hard physical labor, propagation, and defense. We conjecture that the elderly were a vital link to the past. Before printing presses and computers, the only way to store lessons of survival was in the recollections of those who had experienced crises, threats from enemies, natural disasters—and survived. Archives and libraries reposed in peoples' memories. The same would likely be true of myths and religious rituals, which could be transmitted to novitiates only by those versed in their complexity.

Today the elderly play no such role in society and consequently enjoy no such honors. Rather, they are objects of patronizing debate regarding the proper allocation of responsibility and resources for their care. The best hope the elderly have is that the debate will be "compassionate," that as hapless victims and refugees in the war between the elderly and the young and between the haves and the have-nots, they will be treated humanely.

For today to be both elderly and poor is to have two reasons for being socially extraneous and burdensome. The elderly, says the philosopher Daniel Callahan in a book entitled *Setting Limits*[3]—a term parents use on pets and fractious toddlers—are not "socially *indispensable* in the way that children and young adults are for a society" (his emphasis). Although the book is a deeply sympathetic examination of the role of the elderly in society, it inescapably confirms the underlying assumption of its title—namely, that in this time of spiraling health-care costs, the elderly are being indulged. It is a view most people are unwilling to acknowledge and Callahan has been roundly criticized for impoliticly exposing. Yet, ironically, the fact that we, as a nation, contribute so generously to the elderly's welfare may actually be a measure of our compassion. For you see, as opposed to ancient societies, we have so little use for them. Merely look around and you can see that youth rules today: loud music; flamboyant fashions; glossy magazines; iPods; brash, unreflective, iconoclastic movies and television; and general impatience. Any hope that the musings of the elderly might be heard, much less taken seriously, even much less considered vital to society's survival or religious significance suggests delusions of grandeur. Yet one can't help wondering what they would prefer: to be supported on grounds of compassion or—as were Baucis and Philemon—on the grounds of social necessity?

Finally, the ancient Greek story asserts a timeless communal ethic. Jupiter and Mercury, presenting as weary travelers, were rejected by all the village inhabitants until they were welcomed by Baucis and Philemon. In ancient societies, which lacked organized charities, welfare systems, and various forms of disability insurance, health insurance, and unemployment insurance, the individual relied (like Blanche DuBois) "on the kindness of strangers." It should be no puzzle that inhospitality was harshly punished. A lonely traveler had only those limited means for survival that the landscape afforded. Life could depend on it. In a time of precarious nature and capricious fortune, each person was utterly beholden to the good will and charity of others. This is something the healthy and vigorous learn when they get sick and the young learn when they get old. Like any other doctor caring for elderly patients, I realized that nothing

I do in my office compares to what others in the community do outside. Without follow-up care, all the most miraculous medicine and surgery will fail. How sad that the elderly must suffer until society makes this discovery—that it is the devotion of the community the elderly require more than the virtuosity of any one individual.

The perpetual debate over efforts to revise Medicare illustrates this problem and, sadly, seems to reflect the war between the haves and the have-nots and the war between the elderly and the young. Ironically, the usual protests against plans to "privatize" the system are not directed at the failure to examine, much less deliver, the kind of medical care the elderly want, or the kind of care the elderly need, or anything else that has to do with the health of the elderly, but rather because it is another annoying expense in the federal budget that has to be fiddled with and reduced one way or another.

What would Jupiter and Mercury have made of our government's inhospitality? Would they have ordained that it "**pay the penalty of its impiety**"? If our country suffers a similar fate of that wracked village before the eyes of some wondering Baucis and Philemon—perhaps an ever deeper immersion in divisive social and economic bitterness—it could be because we failed to heed the lessons of this ancient myth.

REFERENCES

1. *Bulfinch's Mythology: The Age of Fable of Stories of Gods and Heroes* by Thomas Bulfinch. New York: Crown Publishers, Inc., 1978, originally published 1855.
2. Finley, M.I. *The World of Odysseus.* London: The Folio Society, 2002.
3. Callahan, D. *Setting Limits: Medical Goals in an Aging Society.* New York: Simon & Schuster, 1987.

CHAPTER SIX

Hoping for a Miracle

Baby Agnes (name changed) was a premature infant born to a fundamentalist Christian couple. The baby suffered severe brain injury during her delivery as a result of lack of oxygen when she choked on the thick, tenacious material (called meconium) that accumulates in the fetal intestine and sometimes spills out into the surrounding fluid while the baby is still in the mother's womb.

The physicians in the neonatal ICU immediately set to work rescuing her, suctioning her and resuscitating her repeatedly. Baby Agnes survived, but despite all their efforts she remained unresponsive to her environment except for marked irritability and recurrent seizures. In an attempt to control the seizures, the physicians prescribed high doses of anticonvulsive medication while closely monitoring her blood pressure.

Over the next several days, everyone who observed the newborn's many grimaces and seizures thought she was probably suffering, and all the consultants agreed the brain damage was so severe she was unlikely to improve.

The physician most involved with her treatment went to the family and recommended that further efforts to prolong life be discontinued and only comfort care measures be given. The family, who unceasingly kept an eye on everything the nurses did, strongly objected. Instead of sedatives and narcotics, and tranquilizers (which could increase the risk of death), they demanded that all life-sustaining treatments, including CPR, be carried out in hopes of a "miracle." They brought in members of their religious congregation who supported them in their treatment demands. The care team was torn between their compassion for the infant and their desire to honor the parents' hopes for a miracle.

What does it mean to hope for a miracle?

It used to be that when people sought a miracle they went to church and prayed to God. Now they enter the hospital and demand it of physicians. This is ironic, because to seek a miracle literally means to lay aside human efforts and turn to God. Indeed the very meaning of miracle depends on the notion that "the things which are impossible with men are possible with God." [Luke 18:27] In Gospel stories, it is Jesus and his disciples, not doctors, who perform acts of healing, so that "the blind see, the lame walk, the lepers are cleansed, the deaf hear, the dead are raised."[Luke 7:22] These miracles are achieved not by medical treatments but by prayer, laying on of hands, revelation, and faith. As for physicians, they can do no more than nature allows.

In this case, Baby Agnes's parents were motivated by spiritual factors and would not be persuaded by appeals to facts and statistics. Her physician spent several hours going over the opinions of the specialists, all of whom supported the physician's prognosis and treatment plan. But the parents were not swayed.

The physician then requested an ethics consultation. As the consultant, I met with the family, but it was clear that they had heard it all and had no intention of changing their mind. Again, like the other members of the health-care team, I was moved by the infant's apparent distress. We could see that despite the medication, the infant struggled and went into seizures whenever the nurses attempted to suction her respiratory secretions or change her intravenous lines.

I then arranged a follow-up meeting with the full ethics committee, which included hospital and community members. The parents were invited to bring to the meeting any family members and church members they wished. Before the full committee, the infant's physicians reviewed her condition and prognosis in detail, and the parents presented their hopes for divine intervention. The ethics committee expressed concerns about whether the parents were acting in the best interests of the infant, and although the nurses in particular wanted urgent action because of the infant's suffering, the committee, in an effort to respect and reasonably accommodate the family's religious beliefs, recommended that life-sustaining treatments be continued for another week. During this time, the committee offered to meet further with the parents in hopes of resolving the dispute, but the parents refused.

A week passed (a distressing week for all of us) before the ethics committee met again and reviewed the case. This time they voted unanimously to support the physician's proposed change in treatment from aggressive life-sustaining treatment to maximal comfort care. The parents were informed of this decision and were given an additional week to explore the options to transfer the infant to another institution or pursue legal action to compel treatment.

They did neither, and after a week Baby Agnes was provided maximal comfort care and allowed to die during an episode of cardiac failure.

After the infant's death, an attorney representing the parents subpoenaed her medical records. Everyone waited uneasily while the hospital prepared to defend the physicians' actions. The hospital's lawyers were prepared to argue that the physicians had adhered to the highest standard of care, serving the infant's best interests while providing a reasonable—the nurses would have said unreasonable—accommodation of the parents' wishes in an open and fair process. As it turned out a lawsuit was never pursued. Unfortunately, we were never able to discuss this case with the family again.

Fortunately, these are uncommon events. Most families, guided by the health-care team with sensitivity, attentiveness, and patience, come to terms with the limits of medicine and the inevitability of death. But there are those who demand aggressive life-prolonging medical treatments, who place their hopes not in reason or science but in a particular scriptural interpretation, not in the possibilities of nature but in miracles. (A physician who practiced in the Bible Belt once told me: "My patients, they all want to go to heaven— they just don't want to go there from the ICU.")

From a medical perspective, treatments like CPR and mechanical ventilation were never intended to prolong a lingering death—or a body in the state of death—but rather to rescue patients with temporary, reversible life-threatening emergencies. Nevertheless, physicians sometimes find themselves forcing air into the lungs of patients who are permanently unconscious or who have end-stage cancer or applying electrical shocks to feeble, terminally failing hearts in situations that are futile or even cruel.

What then should be the relationship of religious beliefs and goals to medical duties and goals? Does one set of values override the other set of values?

The answer is maybe. Yes, physicians are ethically and legally bound to honor religious freedom insofar as they cannot force unwanted treatments on any competent person. Adult Jehovah's Witness patients, for example, can refuse life-saving blood transfusions for themselves. But they cannot withhold life-saving transfusions from their children. Honoring religious freedom does not require—or even permit—physicians to perform genital mutilation on young girls in accordance with a religious sect, nor to withhold lifesaving surgery from children of Christian Scientists. There are clear limits established by law. As the U.S. Supreme Court said: "Parents may be free to become martyrs themselves. But it does not follow they are free, in identical circumstances, to make martyrs of their children before they have reached the age of full and legal discretion when they can make that choice for themselves."[1]

From the time of Hippocrates, the doctor's goal has been to "assist nature" to *heal* (which means "to make whole") the *patient* (which comes from the word "to suffer"). The Hippocratic physician acknowledged the limits of nature and shunned claims of miraculous cures to avoid the taint of charlatanism. Even today, we must acknowledge that medicine has great powers, but not unlimited powers; physicians have important obligations, but not unlimited obligations. These form the bases for professional standards of practice.

All professions assert their goals and standards, their obligations and limits on obligations. And just as U. S. educators have refused to teach Creationism in science classes as demanded by religious fundamentalists, so, in my opinion, should U. S. physicians resist unreasonable treatment demands by those who seek

92

miraculous cures. In my view, if physicians attempt to do whatever a patient or family wants, the medical profession can no longer claim to be a healing profession dedicated to caring for the sick. Rather it becomes just another commercial enterprise trying to please its customers and charging what the market will bear.

Not all demands for a miracle are made by people who consider themselves religious. Emile Broglie (not his real name) was a 75-year-old man with a history of insulin-dependent diabetes mellitus, hypertension, renal insufficiency, and coronary artery disease associated with frequent episodes of congestive heart failure. He had been rushed to the emergency department in severe respiratory distress and immediately transferred to the ICU. There he experienced a prolonged cardiac arrest that (like Terri Schiavo's; see Chapter 2) was overcome with great difficulty— his brain was severely starved of oxygen-bearing blood, which destroyed his cerebral cortex. For the next 3 years he remained hospitalized and unconscious while his wife remained at his bedside awaiting his miraculous recovery.

Emile Broglie had left no written or verbal instructions indicating his treatment wishes. On the insistence of his wife, he was maintained on life-sustaining treatments, including full code status, mechanical ventilation, renal dialysis, and tube feeding. The doctors and nurses tried to persuade his wife that her husband's prolonged course of life-sustaining treatment in an acute-care hospital was inappropriate. Even while seeking to understand her treatment goals, they expressed their doubts that Emile would want his life sustained in this condition, pointing out that prior to his latest admission to the hospital he had repeatedly resisted coronary bypass surgery and refused renal dialysis.

Emile's wife angrily rejected these suggestions. She declined religious counseling, and insisted that their insurance entitled them to any treatments she wanted because it was "all paid for." Meanwhile, she closely monitored every contact with her husband and demanded and received veto power over which nurses would be assigned to the patient. Many nurses became upset at what they were required to do, and several quit.

Over the years, the care providers made many efforts to resolve the dispute through team meetings, ethics consultations, and meetings of the full ethics committee involving a variety of professional and lay representatives and an experienced mediator. They also tried repeatedly to transfer Emile to a long-term care hospital, but his wife refused, threatening to take legal action and to contact the media. Finally, the physicians announced their determination to withdraw life-sustaining treatments on grounds that they were futile, since the permanently unconscious man was incapable of experiencing any benefit from them. But the hospital administration, in the face of the wife's threats—a lawsuit and "bad headlines"—refused to support them.

It was at this time that the hospital ethics committee requested that I be brought in to see whether I could help. I will eliminate the suspense and admit right away that I could not. But the story still remains instructive.

The hospital administration decided to contract with a professional mediator, someone who had promoted his expertise in medical dispute resolution. From my own experience with Mrs. Broglie, I predicted that this approach would be useless. And indeed, after 2 months of effort, the mediator triumphantly produced a written agreement that made no change in the aggressive course of treatment, with the minor exception that Mrs. Broglie said that she would not demand that chest compressions be part of a resuscitation attempt—an exception she simply ignored every time Emile experienced a cardiac arrest. At long last, Emile died, but only after several more months of mechanical ventilatory support, tube feeding, dialysis, multiple courses of antibiotics, blood pressure support, and rib-cracking resuscitation attempts for repeated episodes of cardiac arrest.

In this case the patient's wife did not invoke any supernatural authority to justify her demand that doctors continue her husband's life-sustaining treatments in hopes of a miracle, nevertheless he was just as implacable as the family in Baby Agnes' case. As far as we could tell, there was no hidden agenda, which often lurks in the shadows of these kinds of demands, such as a pension that the wife has grown accustomed to, which would terminate with the death of the patient. Rather it seemed that Mrs. Broglie's life had become so invested in her husband that she was unable to imagine a life without him, even in his insensate condition. In other words, it was her own needs that were at stake, and it was irrelevant how hard we argued for the needs of the patient himself. Her only goal in life was to have her husband miraculously restored to her.

Where do families get the idea that medicine can achieve miracles and the hospital is the place to go to collect them? It is easy to round up the usual suspects—television, tabloids, slick "health" magazines, and all the other purveyors of sensationalized and fictionalized journalism. Yet, I wondered how much of the blame should fall on the medical establishment itself? From the "miracle drug" era of the 1950s, through the introduction of CPR, artificial kidney machines, and ICUs in the 1960s, through the 1970s and 80s, characterized by dramatic advances in cancer chemotherapy and organ transplantation, medicine has enthusiastically (and justifiably) trumpeted seemingly miraculous treatments that offered rapid cures for diseases previously fatal or, at best, dreadfully long in resolution.

Physicians recognize, of course, that not all treatments achieve "miracles." Some expectations are simply beyond the limits of nature and the powers of even the most modern technology. But I couldn't help wondering: Are physicians and other health-care providers—particularly hospital spokespersons—acknowledging such limits openly? Or are they beginning to exploit unrealistic public expectations in what has become an increasingly competitive health-care environment?

My curiosity was aroused enough after the Baby Agnes episode to get in touch with all 43 of the nation's children's hospitals. I asked them to send me the promotional and informational publications, such as magazines, brochures, or pamphlets, they distribute to the lay public. Sharyn Manning, my assistant at the time, and I carefully and independently read through the 38 batches we received. We looked for articles, case reports, or feature stories that described that hospital's accomplishments or potential benefits of medical treatments in terms of "miracles." Meanwhile we looked for articles, case reports, or feature stories that provided some balance to these expectations—namely, by frankly acknowledging the likelihood of impending limits in the future because of inevitable rationing and resource allocation.[2]

In the 38 publications, we found 8 articles that hailed the accomplishments of the hospital in terms of "miracles." These were usually stories of infants and children described as terminal, incurable, not likely to survive, or given up for dead, who, through the dramatic intervention of the hospital staff, made a remarkable recovery.

The most blatant example of hyperbole was the hospital that described itself in bold type on the cover of its slick magazine as the place "Where Miracles Happen." Other representative quotes were: "Every day there are three or four miracles here [spoken by a nurse];" "We're gearing up for another year of miracles for children [in the first page letter by the hospital's president and chief executive officer];" "The happy kids and families at the reunion are a reminder of the miracles brought about by this special blend of technology and tender loving care [in a feature article];" "Thanks to the skills of Children's pediatric experts, little Alfredo is alive and well. With your continued support, we can help make miracles like Alfredo's happen every day [in a feature story];" and "Miracle stories like Anders will be featured during this year's Children Miracle Network Telethon [in a feature story ending with a plea for contributions]." Promotional articles like the last, advertising a forthcoming "Miracle Network" television program, in which most children's hospitals participate, were ubiquitous. Three hospitals, in addition to the 8 hospitals noted earlier, made reference to the "Miracle Network" television program.

Of the 38 hospitals, 17 had articles that referred to the current health-care environment in terms of limited resources, impending reorganization, rationing, and resource allocation. This would seem to be an impressive number. However, all but three articles emphasized not the possibility of limitations on available health care, but the importance of the hospital's need for more money and resources to increase its competitiveness in order to maintain its ability to deliver more miracles.

Is it surprising that people expect miracles from medicine when those expectations are being nourished not only by the popular media but by medicine itself?

Again, I point out that these intractable cases in which patients demand the impossible rarely proceed to this extreme. Most families come to accept the inevitable death of a loved one. But when they do not, the impact can be devastating. Remember the case of Terri Schiavo, described in Chapter 2, with the acrimonious and prolonged battle between her husband, who wanted to remove her feeding tube and let her die, in accordance with what he perceived to be her wishes, and her parents who refused to let her die. The parents declared, before the astonished judge, that if it were necessary to keep their daughter alive they would even go so far as to demand the amputation of all her limbs. At that point the judge, who had devoted indefatigable attention to both parties, must have become convinced that Terri's parents no longer could be regarded as representing her wishes or best interests.

As in the case of Baby Agnes, great efforts were devoted to the process of mediation to resolve the conflict with Mrs. Broglie. Why was I so skeptical about recruiting a professional mediator to attempt this form of dispute resolution with her? Some have argued that mediation, which has proved valuable in resolving legal disputes, is the solution to resolving disputes in the medical setting. Indeed, during a public meeting I attended, one eminent professor of law expressed outrage that the courts had granted permission for Terri Schiavo's life-sustaining feeding tube to be removed over the objections of her parents. Her feeding tube should not have been removed, the professor declared, until mediation had succeeded in bringing all the parties to agreement, seemingly oblivious to the entrenched positions of the contending parties for over a dozen years. (I later learned that the eminent professor had not the slightest exposure to clinical medicine to support his opinion, had never attended a single patient-care conference, and thus had no personal experience with what actually goes on in these kinds of conflicts.)

Not that we don't always attempt mediation in ethics consultations. Who would not prefer agreement, concord, and harmony? In fact, it is standard practice (and inscribed in many hospital policies) to urge the parties involved in any conflict to follow step-by-step dispute resolution procedures. These include assessing goals, clarifying information, acknowledging differences in values, and arriving at a compromise through negotiation. But as these cases illustrate, compromise is not always attainable in the medical setting.

Dispute resolution, it is worth noting, has its origins in business and the law, where disputes are more likely to involve not life and death but money and property, where a compromise may be accepted, albeit grudgingly, as the best possible outcome.[3] Disputants in these arenas can be persuaded that getting less than everything they want now is a better deal than taking a risk at losing everything they want at some future date. However, there can be no such compromise for people seeking a medical miracle. For the parents of Baby Agnes and for Mrs. Broglie, there was no acceptable tradeoff. As far as they were concerned, their wishes were followed or not followed; their loved one was either alive or dead.

Were the efforts devoted to prolonging the miserable life of Baby Agnes and the insensate life of Emile Broglie consistent with the goals of medicine? The physicians did not think so. What *are* the goals of medicine? And who decides? As with any profession, the duties and limits of the medical profession must be endorsed by the society it serves. However, it begins with physicians stating clearly: "There are things we ought to do and things we ought not do." At some point in a serious and terminal illness, the choice for a physician is not whether the patient will die but how that patient will die. At that point the emphasis on the physician's duty shifts. Will it be a good death or a bad death? Because, in the end, all parties have to compromise with the inevitability of death. I will pursue this difficult issue—what are the goals of medicine and what are the physician's obligations and limits on obligations—in greater detail when I introduce the concept of medical futility in Chapter 8. But before that, let's consider what could possibly be wrong with hoping for a miracle.

REFERENCES

1. *Prince v. Massachusetts,* 321 U.S. 158 (1944.)
2. Manning S, Schneiderman, LJ. Miracles or limits: what message from the medical marketplace? *HEC Forum* (1996) 8(2): 103–8.
3. Schneiderman LJ, Fein JE. The limits of dispute resolution. *Hastings Center Report* (2001) 31(6): 10–1.

CHAPTER SEVEN

What Could Be Wrong
with Hope?

One of the darkest jokes in medicine goes like this:

> Question: "Why do they put those heavy concrete slabs
> on top of graves?"
> Answer: "To keep out the oncologists (cancer specialists)."

It's no secret to the world at large that different specialties in medicine appeal to different personality types. Without going into details, we all have observed that surgeons tend to be "aggressive." They wade in where others fear to tread in the belief that they can get rid of the "badness." They are aggressive optimists. And oncologists? They are at the top of the pile in aggressive optimism, which explains the joke. They almost never want to give up. They are interminable purveyors of hope. Hence, according to the joke, they would even attempt CPR on a buried corpse.

One day, when I was supervising a conference of medical residents on the ethics of critical care decision-making, we went over a variety of published clinical research articles. We all agreed that the empirical studies showed that hospitalized patients with metastatic cancer had a negligible chance of surviving a cardiac arrest, no matter how much effort was devoted to resuscitation. So, we agreed, instead of forcing a treatment on patients that was only going to cause more pain and suffering, it would be far better to write a DNAR (Do Not Attempt Resuscitation) order to emphasize comfort care. At that point, one of the residents asked in bewilderment: "Then how come all the patients with metastatic cancer on the cancer service are full code?" I suggested she ask her attending physician. The answer the medical resident returned with the following session was not heartening. It's the only way to make sure the patient won't be neglected, her attending told her. How sad, I thought, that the choices being taught to this young physician were limited to neglect or torture. I will deal with this impoverished view of medical care in greater detail in Chapter 9.

Like many doctors, I am often asked by friends who have been presented with a treatment plan by their doctor to render a second—more usually a fourth or fifth—opinion. Probably the most difficult situation I faced was when a close friend, Brenda (not her real name), a professional musician, who while feeling perfectly well was discovered to have early stage metastatic breast cancer. Her oncologist urged her to undergo a combined procedure that was the height of fashion at the time. First she would receive high-dose chemotherapy in an extreme effort to kill off all the cancer cells throughout the body; then she would receive bone marrow transplantation. An unavoidable severe side effect of the first phase—in addition to the nausea, vomiting, fever, diarrhea, and extreme weakness—is that it would obliterate all her bone marrow cells, the precursors to vital red and white blood cells and platelets. This would make her vulnerable to life-threatening infections, anemia, and bleeding for several weeks, until replacement bone marrow could be successfully implanted and replenish those circulating cells.

Oncologists were promoting this treatment combination–which had been shown to be effective for hematologic malignancies like leukemia–for metastatic breast cancer. But there was no reliable evidence from randomized controlled trials to justify its use for the latter condition—a very different solid tumor. This did not seem to matter. Many leading oncologists were so convinced of the treatment's efficacy that they dismissed—even opposed—pleas by skeptical physicians to carry out such definitive research. They even joined in demanding that insurance companies and managed care organizations pay for this treatment when these organizations refused on the grounds that their contracts excluded "experimental," by which they meant unproven, treatments.

I pointed out to Brenda and her husband the lack of supporting evidence for this harsh treatment. But it was not an opinion they wanted to hear. She, like other women, almost without exception, chose to follow the optimistic predictions of her oncologist. He gave her hope.

Brenda underwent the procedure, experienced many of the severe risks—she nearly died of overwhelming sepsis and loss of blood—and survived a few more years, during which time the cancer returned. She also developed a form of leukemia believed to have been a consequence of the high-dose chemotherapy before she died.

Okay, Brenda died, but how do we know she wouldn't have died sooner if she had not undergone the treatment? Two things happened: one long overdue, the other disgraceful. The long overdue: At last responsible researchers set out to perform randomized controlled trials. These showed conclusively that there was no advantage to having women undergo this highly toxic form of treatment for metastatic breast cancer rather than the conventional protocols of chemotherapy, whether measured as days of life or quality of life. The disgraceful: One researcher who had claimed to show a benefit was found to have fabricated his data.

How did such a thing happen in the context of modern, science-based medicine? The answer, I'm afraid, is expressed in that one word: Hope.

It is one of the most entrenched commandments in medicine: "Never take away a patient's hope!"—which is invariably interpreted to mean never take away a patient's hope for miraculous life-saving cures. Often it is issued during the treatment of a terminally ill patient to spur and justify the continuation of extreme life-prolonging efforts. Hope has been called one of a patient's "most powerful internal resources,"[1] and "a powerful ally, our last defense against despair."[2] One prominent physician confidently stated: "communicating hope can improve patients' prognosis."[3]

Others claim that hope, optimism, and a "will to live" prolong life.[4,5] Even unrealistically optimistic beliefs, one group of researchers declared, might be life-prolonging.[8] By contrast, a sense of hopelessness about the future is alleged to increase mortality,[6] and a self-described "realistic acceptance" in patients with AIDS is assumed to shorten survival time.[7]

Alas, when one carefully scrutinizes the facts and statistics, none of these claims stand up with respect to serious illness.[9,10] One group of English researchers, after initially claiming that survival rates in patients with breast cancer were linked to a hopeful outlook,[11] later retracted that claim after performing a larger and more detailed study.[12] Other researchers looked for and found no evidence of a connection between several highly touted psycho-social factors, including hope, and improved survival in advanced cancer.[13] Similarly, after another careful empirical study, re-searchers concluded that there is "little scientific basis for the popular lay and clinical belief that psychological coping styles have an important influence on overall or event-free survival in pa-tients with cancer." They further cautioned: "People with cancer should not feel pressured into adopting particular coping styles to improve survival or reduce the risk of recurrence."[14] An editor of the *New England Journal of Medicine,* Marcia Angell, stated bluntly that "our belief in disease as a direct reflection of mental state is largely folklore."[15]

Promoting a belief in the medical value of hope[16,17] inevitably imposes on the physician contradictory obligations: to maintain hope while at the same time maintaining honesty. Patients them-selves may impose this contradictory demand. In one study, patients with terminal cancer who were receiving hospice-type palliative care unanimously stated they preferred that their doc-tors be "honest." Meanwhile more than 90% said they wanted their doctors to be "optimistic."[18] How to achieve this? Easy, said one physician. Tell the truth "in the most optimistic way."[3]

Of course, if hope really is a beneficial or—at worst—a harmless psychological state that enables patients to cope with profound life challenges, there would be little reason to deny it. What could be wrong with hope? Well, what about the possibility that hope might actually cause harm?

Several writers have expressed concerns that this might be the case—if hope is false or unreasonable. For example, unreasonable hope by the physician or the patient or the parents of a child in the face of imminent death might deprive the patient of more beneficial palliative care.[20,21,22,23] (See Chapter 9.) If false or unreasonable hope for a cure delayed a referral to a hospice, the patient might endure needless suffering; meanwhile, hospice physicians and nurses would have "inadequate time to learn [a patient's] needs and develop an optimal plan for care."[24] So-called "optimistic bias," the tendency to believe that one is immune from laws of chance, might "seriously hinder efforts to promote risk-reducing behaviors."[25] "Highly optimistic" patients, who are "less likely to report being bothered by symptoms,"[26] might tend to ignore or deny early symptoms of cancer and thus lose the chance to obtain curative treatment.[10] Finally, one writer points out, the cost of false hope is "not only the physical and emotional agony of dying patients who try last-ditch, occasionally unproven treatments, but also the depletion, financially and psychologically, of the patients' survivors."[19]

These are speculative concerns. Are there facts and statistics—empirical evidence—to support them? The answer is yes. In one study of over 1,000 patients at several different hospitals, researchers looked at what happened to critically ill patients whose own prognostic estimates exceeded their physicians' prognostic estimates—in other words, patients who were more hopeful. These patients demanded many more aggressive and invasive life-sustaining treatments, including CPR and mechanical ventilation, than did patients with more realistic estimates of their prognoses. The increased use of these treatments did not improve their hospital survival in the slightest. It only increased their suffering.[27,28]

Grasping at hope is understandable, of course—patients want to be cured. Unfortunately, most patients obtain their hope from dubious sources, particularly television and the misinformation highway known as the Internet. For example, success rates for CPR on popular shows like "ER," "Chicago Hope," and "Rescue 911" are significantly higher than the most optimistic survival rates in the medical literature.[29] And several studies have shown that elderly patients who request CPR in the event of cardiac arrest have an inflated view of its ease and success. When such patients are informed about the true nature of the technique and the probability of survival, their desire for the procedure plummets.[30,31]

Lack of knowledge and denial, perhaps "reinforced unwittingly by the physician," (said one researcher) may also account for unrealistic hope of cure and belief in quack therapies by many patients with metastatic cancer[32] (see Chapter 10).

Studies of physician behavior have led to contradictory findings. Several research groups have reported that physicians hold more pessimistic prognoses than do their seriously ill patients. [33,34,35,36] Other researchers found physicians to be overly optimistic.[37,38,39] As you can imagine, such variations in the framing of decisions and prognostic estimates by physicians—based on optimistic or pessimistic beliefs, lots of hope or little hope—naturally would lead patients toward more or less aggressive courses of action, which would have significant consequences on diagnostic strategies, health-care utilization, and costs.[40,41,42]

Physicians sometimes intentionally mislead their patients, usually by being unduly optimistic.[42,43,44] For example, 86% of internists responding to a national survey expressed the view that it was best to have an "upbeat attitude" with patients; 75% reported that they sometimes found it helpful "to shade prognoses to the positive;" and 64% reinforced patient optimism, as opposed to only 5% who stated that they reinforced patient pessimism.[43]

Several explanations have been offered for this tendency to accentuate the positive, including a reluctance "to acknowledge that patients they know well are close to death;" "ego bias"—namely, a "systematic overestimation of the prognosis of one's own patients compared with the expected outcome of a population of similar patients;" and "enthusiasm for new treatments."[45,46,47]

Also, one cannot discount the embarrassing possibility that an erroneously pessimistic prognosis may make the physician an object of mockery. ("That dumb doc gave me only a month to live, and here I am going strong a year later!")

As we can see, hope is almost always promoted for its impact on a single dimension—life prolongation. In a thoughtful commentary, a nurse, in describing her mother's dying and her "gift—the link between honesty and hope" suggests "we distort the meaning of hope when we make it depend on the possibility of physical survival." She traces this view back to Judaic and Christian traditions.[48] Indeed, one has to wonder whether, as we noted in the previous chapters, the central role of miracles in Christian mythology—sensationalized by many modern evangelists—may not underlie the contemporary expectation, or at least hope, for medical miracles.

An oft-cited testimonial to the life-prolonging effect of hope is Viktor Frankl's description of his experiences in the Nazi concentration camps.[49] However, what Frankl actually propounded was not hope but "man's desire to find and fulfill a meaning in his life, or for that matter in the individual life situations confronting him."[50] He went on to argue that "what underlies the attempt to establish faith, hope, love, and the will by command is the manipulative approach. The attempt to bring these states about at will, however, is ultimately based on an inappropriate objectification and reification of these human phenomena: They are turned into things, into mere objects."[51]

The Australian sociologist Douglas Ezzy explored this notion of hope-as-meaning in the narratives patients with HIV use to make sense of their life-threatening illness.[52] Drawing on interviews with patients and a variety of narrative theorists, he defines three categories of narratives: *linear restitution, linear chaotic,* and *polyphonic.*

Linear restitution narratives are characterized as clinging to normal life goals and expectations despite the disease. Hope for these patients focuses on specific future objectives, such as seeing a child grow up and get married, and depends on an optimistic bias that empirically derived prognostic probabilities do not apply to them. Their expectation (and hope) is that normal life will go on for many years by means of successful—and sometimes miraculous—medical interventions. These patients, often in unpremeditated collusion with their physicians, maintain their hope by denying the possibility of death.

Linear chaotic narratives, as the name implies, are characterized by anger and despair because their promising, often idealized, life has been fractured and destroyed by illness. These patients have no hope for the future, no explanatory narrative, no simple organizing principle around which to integrate their experience. To them, reality is a meaningless chaos. However, as Ezzy points out, underlying that chaotic narrative is an implied belief in a lost and longed-for linear narrative "as an ideal, or an imagined solution that would resolve the chaos of the present."[51]

Neither of the above two narratives serves their owners well. Seemingly at opposite poles, both are unrealistic in the most important sense and therefore unhelpful. The most beneficial form of hope is based on a *polyphonic* narrative. As the name implies, patients who discover and accept this form of narrative are "many voiced." Rather than focusing on pre-existing milestones, these patients are open to "uncertainty about the future, a more communally oriented morality and politics, and an acceptance of the reality of death at some stage in the future."[52] In discussions with these patients, I have learned how exquisite their pleasure has become in acts they previously took for granted—things that occur in the here-and-now: simply looking up at the sky, inhaling the air, feeling water on their skin, listening to children's voices and watching them play. They experience a new and profound wonder in the presence of these everyday, yet remarkable, phenomena. Their notion of hope seeks "mystery, surprise and creativity."[52]

Paradoxically, I applied this lesson most successfully with a patient whom I will call Sophia Trabant, who was not at the end of life but was suffering almost as though she were. Sofia was a lawyer in her thirties with chronic fatigue syndrome. This is a mysterious ailment that often afflicts hardworking people in the midst of a successful career. Their physical and even mental activities deteriorate so severely that instead of working they desperately lurch from doctor to doctor searching for a cure. The doctors perform all sorts of tests, usually depending on their particular specialty—rheumatology, cardiology, infections disease, endocrinology, neurology, although almost never psychiatry because typically these patients resent hearing that "it's all in the mind." Sophia was referred to me with the hope that maybe one more physician might find something everyone else had missed. When I saw her in my office she was accompanied by an enormous volume containing copies of her medical work-ups. Going through them carefully, I could see that the other physicians had tested her for every conceivable cause for her condition. And her physical examination, including careful neurological and muscle testing, was completely normal. There was nothing I could add—except . . . I reached for an approach to helping her that I later learned comprises what is called cognitive behavioral therapy. I said to her: "I don't doubt you have a very disabling condition that makes you feel tired all the time. And I don't doubt that it is very frustrating to you that medicine can't cure you. But think about this for a moment. What if you had incurable cancer and felt this fatigued? Wouldn't you try to make the most of what little strength you have left, make the most of each day, push yourself to do the most you can do? You wouldn't want to just give in to your fatigue and do nothing. Eventually, the cancer would kill you, so you would be determined to make the most of your remaining life, wouldn't you? You would try to get outside, enjoy your surroundings, push yourself, walk a bit, drive to a restaurant, a movie, a concert. Well, I'm going to ask you to try putting that determination to work with your condition. I can assure you that you won't hurt your body. And even better, this is not a fatal disease. Whatever you can make yourself do to improve your life you can count on being able to do it indefinitely." In short, I tried to redirect her attention away from her limits to her possibilities, things that could still give her pleasure—embracing her mortality. To my pleasure and astonishment (and hers as well), she saw me again a week later, then again and again over several months. And gradually, she "pushed" herself into achieving her own cure—making the most of her life.

I believe that the difficult but essential task for all of us, physicians as well as laypersons, is to discard the conventional, narrow view of hope as a psychological tool to prolong life. That version of hope is useless, if not perilous. Rather, hope should provide a wider illumination. For the physician, that means enlightening (namely, casting light on) the ways we can make the best possible medical decisions to achieve the best possibilities in the life that is left. In the words of Martha Nussbaum, "to comprehend what sort of life one has actually got" and to discover "where the valuable things *for us* are to be found."[53] In other words, helping us to embrace our mortality. Then, when death is inevitable, avoiding futile life-prolonging efforts, and ensuring that the exit will be a good death. Is that not a hope worth hoping for?

REFERENCES

1. Johnson LH, Dahlen R, Roberts SL. Supporting hope in congestive heart failure patients. *Dimensions in Critical Care Nursing* (1997) 16:65–78.
2. Bone RC. Benediction: a farewell to my medical colleagues *The Journal of Critical Illness* (1997) 12(7):139–40.
3. Ubel A. Truth in the most optimistic way. *Annals of Internal Medicine* (2001) 134:1142–3.
4. Maruta T, Colligan RC, Malinchoc M, Offord KP. Optimists vs pessimists: survival rate among medical patients over a 30-year period. *Mayo Clinic Proceedings* (2000) 75:140–3.
5. Levy BR, Slade MD, Kunkel SR, Kasl SV. Longevity increased by positive self-perceptions of aging. *Journal of Personality and Social Psychology* (2002) 83:261–70.
6. Stern SL, Dhanda R, Hazuda HP. Hopelessness predicts mortality in older Mexican and European Americans. *Psychosomatic Medicine* (2001) 63:344–51.
7. Reed GM, Kemeny ME, Taylor SE, Wang H-Y J, Visscher BR. Realistic acceptance as a predictor of decreased survival time in gay men with AIDS. *Health Psychology* (1994)13(4):299–307.

8. Taylor SE, Kemeny ME, Reed GM, Bower JE, Gruenewald TL. Psychological resources, positive illusions, and health. *American Psychologist* (2000) 55(1):99–109.

9. Affleck G, Tennen H. Construing benefits from adversity: adaptational significance and dispositional underpinnings. *Journal of Personality* (1996) 64(4):899–922.

10. Rabkin JG, Ferrando SJ, Lin S-H, Sewell M, McElhiney M. Psychological effects of HAART: a 2-year study. *Psychosomatic Medicine* (2000) 62:413–22.

11. Greer S, Morris T, Pettingale KW. Psychological response to breast cancer: effect on outcome. *The Lancet* (1979) 2:785–7.

12. Watson M, Haviland JS, Greer S, Davidson J, Bliss JM. Influence of psychological response on survival in breast cancer: a population-based cohort study. *The Lancet* (1999) 354:1331–6.

13. Cassileth BR, Lusk EJ, Miller DS, Brown LL, Miller C. Psychosocial correlates of survival in advanced malignant disease? *New England Journal of Medicine* (1985) 312:1551–5.

14. Petticrew M, Bell R, Hunter D. Influence of psychological coping on survival and recurrence in people with cancer: systematic review. *British Medical Journal* (2002) 325:1066–76.

15. Angell M. Disease as a reflection of the psyche. *New England Journal of Medicine* (1985) 312:1570–2.

16. Cutliffe JR, Herth KA. The concept of hope in nursing 5: hope and critical care nursing. *British Journal of Nursing* (2002) 11(18):1190–5.

17. Cutcliffe JR, Herth K. The concept of hope in nursing 1: its origins, background and nature. *British Journal of Nursing* (2002) 11(12): 832–40.

18. Kutner JS, Steiner JF, Corbett KK, Jahnigen DW, Barton PL. Information needs in terminal illness. *Social Science & Medicine* (1999) 48:1341–52.

19. Hoffman J. Doctors' Delicate Balance in Keeping Hope Alive. *The New York Times.* December 24, 2005.

20. Brody H, Lynn J. The physician's responsibility under the new Medicare reimbursement for hospice care. *New England Journal of Medicine* (1984) 310:920–2.

21. Parkes CM. Commentary: Prognoses should be based on proved indices not intuition. *British Medical Journal* (2000) 320:473.

22. Wolfe J, Klar N, Grier HE, et al. Understanding of prognosis among parents of children who died of cancer: impact on treatment goals and integration of palliative care. *Journal of the American Medical Association* (2000) 284:2469–75.

23. Pearlman RA. Inaccurate predictions of life expectancy. *Archives of Internal Medicine* (1988) 148:2537–8.

24. Christakis NA, Escarce JJ. Survival of Medicare patients after enrollment in Hospice programs. *New England Journal of Medicine* (1996) 225:172–78.

25. Weinstein ND, Optimistic biases about personal risks. *Science* (1989) 246:1232–3.

26. Scheier MF, Carver CS. Optimism, coping, and health: assessment and implications of generalized outcome expectancies. *Health Psychology* (1985) 4(3):219–47.

27. Weeks JC, Cook EF, O'Day SJ, et al., relationship between cancer patients' predictions of prognosis and their treatment preferences. *Journal of the American Medical Association* (1998) 279:1709–14.

28. Phillips RS, Wenger NS, Teno J, et al. Choices of seriously ill patients about cardiopulmonary resuscitation: correlates and outcomes. *American Journal of Medicine* (1996) 100:128–37.

29. Diem SJ, Lantos JD, Tulsky JA. Cardiopulmonary resuscitation on television—miracles and misinformation. *New England Journal of Medicine* (1996) 334:1578–82.

30. Murphy DJ, Burrows D, Santilli S, et al. The influence of the probability of survival on patients' preferences regarding cardiopulmonary resuscitation. *New England Journal of Medicine* (1994) 330:545–9.

31. Schonwetter RS, Walker RM, Kramer DR, et al. Resuscitation decision making in the elderly: the value of outcome data. *Journal of General Internal Medicine* (1993) 8:295–300.

32. Eidinger RN, Schapira DV. Cancer patients insight into their treatment, prognosis, and unconventional therapies. *Cancer* (1984) 53: 2736–40.

33. Andrykowski MA, Brady MJ, Greiner CB, et al. "Returning to normal" following bone marrow transplantation: outcomes expectations and informed consent. *Bone Marrow Transplantation* (1995) 15:573–81.

34. Mackillop WJ, Steward WE, Ginsburg AD, Stewart SS. Cancer patients' perceptions of their disease and its treatment. *British Journal of Cancer* (1988) 58:355–8.

35. Lee SJ, Fairclough D, Antin HJ, Weeks JC. Discrepancies between patient and physician estimates for the success of stem cell transplantation. *Journal of the American Medical Association* (2001) 285:1034–8.

36. Arkes HR, Dawson NV, Speroff T, et al. The covariance decomposition of the probability score and its use in evaluating prognostic estimates. *Medical Decision Making* (1995) 15:120–31.

37. Perkins HS, Jonsen AR, Epstein WV. Providers as predictors: using outcome predictions in intensive care. *Critical Care Medicine* (1986) 14(2):105–10.

38. Heyse-Moore LH, JohnsonBell VE. Can doctors accurately predict the life expectancy of patients with terminal cancer? *Palliative Medicine* (1987) 1:165–66.

39. Christakis NA, Lamont EB. Extent and determinants of error in doctors' prognoses in terminally ill patients: prospective cohort study. *British Medical Journal* (2000) 320:469–72.

40. Wilson DK, Kaplan RM, Schneiderman LJ. Framing of decisions and selections of alternatives in health care. *Social Behavior* (1987) 2:51–9.

41. Pearlman RA, Variability in physician estimates of survival for acute respiratory failure in chronic obstructive pulmonary disease. *Chest* (1987) 91(4):515–21.

42. Zimmerman JE, Knaus WA, Sharpe SM, Anderson AS, Draper EA, Wagner DP. The use and implications of do not resuscitate order in Intensive Care Units. *Journal of the American Medical Association* (1986) 25(53):351–6.

43. Christakis NA, Iwashyna TJ. Attitude and self-reported practice regarding prognostication in a national sample of internists. *Archives of Internal Medicine* (1998) 158: 2389–95.

44. Lamont EB, Christakis NA. Prognostic disclosure to patients with cancer near the end of life. *Annals of Internal Medicine* (2001) 134: 1096–105.

45. Smith JL. Commentary: Why do doctors overestimate? *British Medical Journal* (2000) 320:472–3.

46. Poses RM, McClish DK, Bekes C, Scott WE, Morley JN. Ego bias, reverse ego bias, and physicians' prognostic *Critical Care Medicine* (1991) 19(12):1533–9.

47. Lynn J, Teno JM, Harrell FE. Accurate prognostications of death: opportunities and challenges for clinicians. *Western Journal of Medicine* (1995) 163:250–7.

48. Christopher M. My mother's gift—the link between honesty and hope. *Bioethics Forum* (1999) 15(1):5–13.

49. Frankl, V. *Man's Search for Meaning.* Boston: Beacon Press, 1962.

50. Frankl, V. E. *Man's Search for Ultimate Meaning.* Cambridge: Perseus Publishing, 2000: 17.

51. Ibid.

52. Ezzy D. Illness narratives: time, hope and HIV. *Social Science and Medicine* (2000) 50(5):605–17.

53. Nussbaum, M. "Transcending Humanity." *Love's Knowledge.* New York: Oxford University Press, 1990: 381.

CHAPTER EIGHT

Medical Futility

Several years ago, a battered infant I shall call Baby Charlie was admitted to a children's hospital. After more than a month of observation and testing, the physicians concluded that Charlie had been beaten so badly that his brain was almost completely destroyed, leaving him permanently unconscious. Unlike Baby Agnes in Chapter 6, Baby Charlie had *no* reactions to the outside environment. All he had left were his minimal brain stem functions—peristalsis, digestion, respiration, excretion, heartbeat—the so-called "vegetative functions." The physicians wished to withdraw life-sustaining treatment because, in their judgment, the infant would never regain consciousness and therefore would never have the capacity to experience any benefit from being kept alive. However, the mother, who was the prime battery suspect, insisted that Charlie be kept alive. In fact, he could be kept alive for years, even decades, because, except for the devastating brain damage, Baby Charlie was healthy in every other respect.

The hospital had just adopted a policy specifically stating that life-sustaining treatment for permanent unconsciousness was futile for the very reason that the condition foreclosed the possibility of the patient experiencing any medical benefit from that treatment. According to the policy, after suitable subspecialty consultations and deliberations, including efforts to gain parental agreement and documentation of unanimous ethics committee support, the patient's physician had the authority to discontinue life-sustaining treatment on the grounds of "medical futility."

I shall return to describe what finally happened to Baby Charlie, but first: What does it mean to invoke medical futility? Is it a topic that is clarified by the consideration of facts, statistics, empathy, and imagination? I first explored this notion in collaboration with my colleagues Albert Jonsen and Nancy S. Jecker, both of whom are philosophers.

To judge from ancient documents, the concept of medical futility is as old as medicine itself. Physicians have always recognized that sometimes treatments have such a low likelihood of success they should not even be attempted.[1] For example, in the collected writings of a school of physicians led and inspired about 400 B.C. by the legendary Hippocrates, the following statements can be found:

"Whenever the illness is too strong for the available remedies, the physician surely must not expect that it can be overcome by medicine."

"To attempt futile treatment is to display an ignorance that is allied to madness."[2]

Beginning about 15 years ago, the topic of medical futility became a matter of stormy contention in medicine. Some critics even argued that the term "medical futility" should be abandoned altogether.[3] But as one critic acknowledged:

"Those who call for the abandonment of the concept have no substitute to offer. They persist in making decisions with, more or less, covert definitions. The common sense notion that a time does come for all of us when death or disability exceeds our medical powers cannot be denied. This means that some operative way of making a decision when 'enough is enough' is necessary. It is a mark of our mortality that we shall die. For each of us some determination of futility by any other name will become a reality. Some working definition therefore must be recognized by which the criterion of futility can be judged."[4]

In ancient Greece, the *futilis* was a religious vessel that had a wide top and a narrow bottom. The peculiar shape caused the vessel to tip over easily, which made it of no practical use for anything other than ceremonial occasions. This root of "futility" reminds us that words have a metaphoric power as well as a literal meaning. Is it not possible that unrealistic expectations and unreasonable demands for futile treatments, such as attempted CPR in a patient suffering from cancer with barely hours to live, may be expressions of deep needs for some form of rituals in times of grief—like the tipping *futilis?* Have not these actions—subjecting the heart and lungs to the pumping forces of machines—perhaps become modern equivalents of religious ceremonies? Understandably, they serve deep psychological needs of those at the bedside to express their love and reverence. But, as we shall see in the Chapter 9, there are better ways to fill these needs and serve the patients.

Why is it so difficult for some to accept the notion of medical futility? There probably are several reasons:

1. In a time when medical miracles seem to abound nearly every day on television, the notion of medical futility does violence to our characteristic American optimism by forcing us to accept what is considered to be "giving up." Worse, some who debate this topic carelessly use the term "futile care." They fail to recognize how their use of the word "care" arouses resistance in those who interpret it as signifying abandonment by physicians who no longer *care* for their loved one. As we will discuss later and also in the Chapter 9, although a particular *treatment* may be futile, *care* is never futile.

2. In a country in which autonomy and self-determination are promoted as paramount values, for medicine to resist demanded interventions on the grounds that they are not appropriate strikes some critics as a return to the bad old days of physician paternalism and "doctor's orders." Spokespersons for various ethnic and religious groups raise the challenge: If my culture or my religion ordains that a permanently unconscious patient should be kept alive as long as possible, what right does medicine have to set its own professional standards over our values?

   Later in this chapter, I will show how this objection can be dealt with fairly. As I have already noted, other

120

professions—most notably the teaching profession—
stand up for their professional standards when subjected
to outside pressures. And even within the medical profession itself, surgeons make futility decisions every day
simply by refusing requests to operate on a patient
they deem "inoperable."

3. As basic science has become more influential in medical education and the related medical specialties
more powerful, the majority of today's physicians are
trained to focus their attention on the *effects* of treatments on systems and body parts rather than on *benefits* to the overall patient. For example, some critics
argue that a physician should not be entitled to regard
a treatment as futile so long as it can maintain the
function of any part of the body, such as pumping
blood by means of a cardiac pacemaker, moving air by
means of mechanical ventilation, or eliminating wastes
via dialysis, even if the patient is permanently unconscious or in the last agonal moments of a terminal
condition. In short, the instruments of technology are
the focus of attention rather than the patient.

This notion, called "physiologic futility," has been
presented as a "value neutral" definition.[3] However, to
specify physiologic objectives as the goals of medicine is
not value neutral but a value *choice.* That there are those
who seriously advocate this view illustrates to me how
much modern medicine has lost its way, how much it
has become fragmented by subspecialties and technology, and how much it has strayed from its patient-
centered tradition into a brutal version of experimental

physiology. Even worse, this focus on systems and body parts probably has contributed to the cruel neglect of optimal end-of-life care of patients, which the medical profession has only recently discovered and begun to address.

4. In a country in which health-care costs soar while many millions of Americans lack health insurance, there is a confusion between the notion of medical futility (the treatment will provide *no* benefit to a particular patient even though it may be available and cheap) and rationing (the treatment *would* provide a benefit to a particular patient although it may not be available or cheap).[5] This confusion has misled critics into condemning futility as though it were clandestine rationing aimed at minorities and other vulnerable groups. To make matters worse, Americans and their politicians have not come to terms with the necessity that rational choices *will* have to be made if we are ever to have a just society. In short, the best we can hope for is that someday we will have health-care rationing that is decent and fair, which—since it would make no sense—ought not include treatments that are futile. We will discuss health-care rationing in more detail in Chapter 10.

Some critics who reject the notion of futility argue that rationing should determine *all* treatment decisions, that as a matter of policy what physicians do should be determined simply by whatever the customer is willing to pay for. This notion—I'll do anything you want as long as you pay me—would, in my view, lower medicine from a moral profession to a variation on the oldest profession.

(Except that here I have to put in a good word for the oldest profession. Some of my patients have been members of the oldest profession. They assured me there *were* some things they would not do no matter how much they were paid. One can only hope that the medical profession will adhere to such high standards.).

Right now, physicians provide and patients receive treatments in an environment where ad hoc, and often capricious, decisions are rendered. Patients and patients' families have been forced to endure and pay for inhumane, unwanted care either because of individual physician's misguided notions of medical duty or the law or as a result of ill-conceived court decisions. Physicians have practiced "defensive medicine," fearing that anything less than mindless continuation of aggressive treatments would make them legally vulnerable. Consequently, they have given the courts little guidance but to "do everything possible."[6] Medicine, like any profession, must propose its standards of practice, which society can either accept, modify, or reject. This is finally beginning to happen with respect to end-of-life care. The American Medical Association's *Code of Medical Ethics* (1996) in its Guidelines on "Medical Futility in End-of-Life Care" provides an important professional basis for asserting a professional standard.[7] It states that all health-care institutions, large or small, should adopt a policy on medical futility and outlines a step-by-step due process including consultation, efforts at dispute resolution, and, if resolution is unsuccessful, transfer to a willing provider. In the end, the limit to the physician's obligation is clearly stated: If transfer is not possible, the futile treatment need not be offered. (see Appendix for UCSD Medical Center's futility policy.)

Several years ago, I tried to find out whether it was possible to bring hospital policies into a consensus to establish a standard of practice. I convened a conference involving physicians, nurses, lawyers, judges, and a variety of other participants, including ethics committee members from 39 California hospitals.[8] I asked a professor of law, Alex Capron, to help me lead the conference. I chose him to assure that we would be—in the, alas, much maligned phrase—"fair and balanced," because he was an outspoken opponent of medical futility. (As the saying goes, "One can only make peace with one's enemies.")

The conference participants spent an entire day reviewing 26 hospital policies as they applied to specific cases. Nearly all the policies defined futile treatment in terms of patient benefit rather than physiologic effect, and more than half provided specific definitions and examples of clinical conditions that did not warrant life support.

Although the majority of hospitals showed a remarkable degree of agreement, I was disappointed at first that we could not achieve complete unanimity. But we achieved something unexpected and even more remarkable—and respectful of American individuality. Professor Capron pointed out that it is not necessary that there be unanimous agreement to establish a professional standard of practice. The law does not demand unanimity among professionals regarding issues that are matters of professional judgment. Rather, it allows for a "respectable minority"—in this case, hospitals that would agree to provide life-prolonging treatments that the majority of hospitals regard as futile. After all, we already accommodate religious exceptions. We accept that Catholic hospitals do not perform abortions and that some, but not all, hospitals will provide "bloodless" surgery to Jehovah's Witness patients. However, we argued that those hospitals that make no statement that they would limit life-prolonging treatments that the majority of hospitals regard as futile should consider the obligations and actions associated with their position. Is it a position or merely the absence of a position? Specifically, are these hospitals willing to accept the transfer of such a patient? If so, disputes over medically futile treatments could be resolved without requiring hospitals to go to court. Also, it would provide a compassionate service to families with non-mainstream religious beliefs.

Back to Baby Charlie. In dealing with the mother's objection to terminating life-sustaining treatment, the ethics committee members were mindful that the case might serve to test the hospital policy in court, if it came to that. The committee members reasoned that the hospital could anticipate a sympathetic response from a jury because the diagnosis and prognosis were not disputed by any of the medical staff, and it seemed evident that the mother was not acting in her baby's best interests, but only in her own interest—namely, to avoid a murder charge.

Right at that time, however, the U.S. Court of Appeals for the Fourth Circuit handed down an opinion that seemed to support parents who insisted on continuing treatment even when their child's physicians thought it was futile.[9] Twice, the emergency department of a Virginia hospital resuscitated an anencephalic baby (known in the court as Baby K). Anencephaly is a severe and permanent birth defect in which all the brain is missing except for the brain stem—a congenital version of the devastation that had been inflicted on Baby Charlie. The hospital sought a judicial declaration that it was not required to provide respiratory support the next time Baby K returned to its emergency department.

Although Baby K's father and *guardian ad litem* agreed that CPR would be "medically or ethically inappropriate" (the terms used by a state statute that said that physicians were not required to provide such treatments), the court, by a vote of two to one, sided with the mother, who insisted that life support be continued. The court ruled that under the Federal *Emergency Medical Treatment and Active Labor Act* (EMTALA),[10] the hospital had to provide mechanical ventilation for Baby K if that was what it would do for other patients with comparable respiratory problems.[9]

Both Capron and I believe that this was a misapplication of EMTALA, which was really intended to stop hospitals from "dumping" indigent emergency patients. "Even in its weakest moments," the dissenting member of the Fourth Circuit panel said, Congress "would not have attempted to impose federal control in this sensitive, private area." [9]

As it turned out, however, the court's ruling on Baby K was far more limited than originally feared. It did not prohibit physicians from withholding futile or inappropriate treatments. In fact, the Fourth Circuit court itself ruled in a subsequent decision that Baby K concerned only "stabilizing treatment that EMTALA required for a particular emergency medical condition." In other words, every patient in any condition had to be given "stabilizing" treatment while in the emergency department. But once a patient has been admitted, a hospital is not obligated by EMTALA to continue any particular treatment indefinitely. EMTALA, the court ruled, "cannot plausibly be interpreted to regulate medical and ethical decisions outside [the emergency room] context," thus leaving the futility issue to be resolved under state law.[11] Nonetheless, the Baby K decision had a chilling effect on hospitals' willingness to implement futility policies.

For example, shortly after Baby K's case was decided, a lawyer who had helped to write an amicus brief on behalf of the American

Academy of Pediatrics supporting the Virginia hospital's position paid a visit to the children's hospital where Baby Charlie was being kept alive. In the course of our discussion, the lawyer was not entirely thrilled with my critique of the unsuccessful amicus brief. I thought it was badly written and, worse, misleading. Why, I asked, had the brief constantly sought permission from the court to allow the physicians to withhold treatment of Baby K's "respiratory distress?" "Distress" implies suffering. The word was misleading because Baby K couldn't feel a thing. What judge would allow physicians to refuse to treat a patient's "distress?" The term should have been "respiratory failure," signifying that the cardio-respiratory system simply stopped functioning. The lawyer dismissed my objection as irrelevant. (Later I happened to talk to several judges who were familiar with the case. When I explained that Baby K was so devoid of brain structure she had no awareness of anything and therefore could feel no "distress," they invariably responded, "I didn't know that.")

In any event, on the lawyer's advice, the hospital administration rescinded the futility policy and refused to allow the withdrawal of life support on the battered, unconscious Baby Charlie. He died five and a half years later without ever regaining consciousness.

At least one hospital has been willing to terminate life support on the grounds of medical futility, despite objections from the patient's next of kin, and then face a suit for damages in court. Following advice from the chair of the hospital's ethics committee, physicians at the Massachusetts General Hospital overrode the objections of the family of Catherine Gilgunn (a permanently unconscious 71-year-old patient who suffered from many medical complications) and removed her respiratory support. After her death, the patient's daughter, who served as her surrogate decision-maker, sued the hospital and two physicians, but the jury rejected her claim of negligent infliction of emotional suffering.[12]

The jury agreed that the daughter was probably expressing her mother's desire to be kept alive in an unconscious state indefinitely, but they agreed that the hospital had no obligation to carry out that desire. Contrary to the anxieties of so many physicians and hospitals, the jury decision strikes me as providing evidence that society is quite receptive to the notion that physicians are not obligated to provide treatments judged to be futile. This could well have been the jury's decision if the Baby Charlie case had been allowed to go to trial. A lawyer's advice, which was just as faulty as his Baby K amicus brief, prevented it.

Despite the outcome in the *Gilgunn* case, many physicians doubt they will be supported by their institution if they act according to what they perceive to be their professional values. This was strikingly revealed in a survey we conducted of physicians at all 43 children's hospitals in the country after the Baby Agnes and Baby Charlie cases and the Baby K decision.[13] Although the respondents—chairs of the ethics committee and neonatal and emergency department physicians—unanimously condemned the efforts to keep alive the anencephalic Baby K (who survived over 2 years), almost all acknowledged that their own hospital would probably yield to demands for life-sustaining treatment in a similar case because of fears of lawsuits and bad headlines.

I have been involved in more than a dozen ethics consultations involving a conflict over how long to keep a permanently unconscious patient alive (it is estimated there may be as many as 30,000–40,000 such patients being kept alive in our country). One such patient was Raoul Cabrillo (not his real name), a young Mexican in his twenties, who was hit by a U. S. driver while running across the border. He was brought to the hospital, where he remained for over a year, permanently unconscious, and on a surgically implanted feeding tube. Like Terri Schiavo, the 25-year-old woman who remained unconscious through almost 15 years of litigation, although not to as outrageous level of spectacle, Raoul also became a political cause célèbre and his case was debated in Congress. Only when he choked to death on his regurgitated stomach contents did he finally bring the medical—albeit not the legal or political—debate to an end.

Why do we persist in keeping such patients alive? Although reluctance to terminate life support most often may represent nothing more than financial self-interest or fear of litigation, to be fair, we cannot ignore a more morally supportable reason—namely, the concern that social value judgments might decay into egregious public policy killings. This is the feared "slippery slope" argument. Is there a sufficiently compelling counter argument to it? Can we find a way to justify that shortening the life of a permanently unconscious patient is not merely dubiously permissible, but that it is ethically obligatory?

Consider the patient in intractable pain from advanced metastatic cancer. Today, there is general medical agreement that—barring patient preferences to the contrary—it is a greater act of beneficence, and therefore the physician's duty, to alleviate suffering, even if the patient's life is thereby shortened.[14,15] Can this rationale be applied to the patient in the persistent vegetative state? Can withdrawing tube feeding, for example, be justified by the intent to alleviate suffering? Ironically, this line of argument is confounded by the very authorities who advocate treatment withdrawal. If it is true, as neurologists claim, that pain and suffering are attributes of consciousness requiring cerebral cortical functioning,

129

then patients who are permanently and completely unconscious cannot experience these symptoms.[16] How then, opponents ask, can medicine justify ending a life that is incapable of suffering?

We cannot *know,* of course, that permanently unconscious patients like Terri Schiavo or Raoul Cabrillo do not suffer. We observe none of the customary signs of awareness, recognition, emotions, thoughts, or any other cognitive mental activity.[16] We can only surmise what, if anything, they are experiencing based on observations we make of external manifestations that correspond to inner states (so we are told) in conscious people. The patient does not smile or frown in acknowledgment of spoken words or music—therefore, we have assumed up to now that the patient is deriving no meaning or satisfaction from these stimuli. (Recently, functional magnetic resonance imaging has provided a view of *internal* manifestations. For example, a 23-year-old woman who remained unresponsive for 5 months following a motor vehicle accident was found to have areas of apparent neural responses to spoken words, even while showing no outward signs of awareness.[17] But was she suffering? We do not know and cannot draw conclusions from the manifestations of brain activity described in this woman, because, as it turned out, she was not permanently unconscious by neurological criteria but was evolving into a minimal conscious state.)

The clinical diagnosis of "permanent vegetative state" following traumatic brain injury is not made until a year has passed for the very reason that a rare patient has "awakened" as late as that.[18] These patients who recover consciousness following a prolonged vegetative state invariably remain severely incapacitated in a locked-in, completely immobilized state or like Mr. Wendland (see Chapter 2) in what is called the minimal conscious state, unable to communicate meaningfully or function purposefully. This raises the question: What has been accomplished? Does this increased level of awareness involve greater suffering for the patient over no awareness at all?

Even if we are forced to acknowledge that we cannot be certain that the absence of consciousness is associated with suffering, can we nonetheless conclude that the patient exists in a state so undesirable that it is perhaps worse than death? If so, then it would be morally permissible to end that state.

Here we have to exercise our empathy and imagination. What do we know about the patient who is permanently unconscious? Only that he or she is isolated from any form of communication—as though exiled or banished from society. Whether or not the patient is capable of perceiving this experience as suffering, isolation of this sort has long been regarded as punishment equal to, if not worse than, death.

From the earliest known time, human beings have functioned as organic components within a community, connected to family, friends, work, rituals, customs, duties, and entertainments. One of the harshest penalties the community could impose was to force a person apart from these connections. In ancient societies, including Greece and Rome, death or banishment was the retribution for capital crimes. If anything, banishment in an era when strangers were equated with enemies (the Latin word was the same for both) made death more miserable.[19] In both Greece and Rome, the notion that came to be expressed as *vita activa* denoted active engagement in the world of men and man-made things. To the Romans, "to live" and "to be among men" *(inter homines esse)* were synonymous.[20]

Aristotle wrote:

"No one would choose to have every conceivable good thing on condition that he remain solitary, for man is a political creature, designed by nature to live with others."[21]

Does this mean that the terror of exile disappeared along with pagan culture and Aristotelian philosophy? History suggests otherwise; for despite the rising status of the solitary and individuated person, banishment for capital crimes persisted throughout Early Christian society. Indeed, along with burning at the stake, it served as punishment for heresy, thus apparently deemed equivalent to the most painful death. (Both penalties also served to get rid of a troublemaker.)

Throughout the Middle Ages and beyond, legends of the Wandering Jew and the Flying Dutchman (men condemned to an eternity of exile) testify to the enduring fear of isolation from society, a condition Shakespeare has the banished Mowbrey describe to his Elizabethan audience as "speechless death" and "solemn shades of endless night"—descriptions surely fitting the persistent vegetative state.[22]

Nor for Romeo is there any doubt that banishment is worse than death:

"Banishment! Be merciful, say 'Death';
   For exile hath more terror in his look, Much more than death: do not say 'banishment.'"[23]

And what about contemporary attitudes? Wars and social upheavals continue to uproot masses of refugees from their homelands and societies. The anguish caused by these forced exiles is well-known, as are the wars and social upheavals they perpetuate.

Primo Levi, recalling his concentration camp experience, almost certainly speaks for many others:

> "The Jews, enemies by definition, impure and sowers of impurity, destroyers of the world, were forbidden that most precious communication, contact with their country of origin and their families: whoever has experienced exile, in any of its many forms, knows how much one suffers when this nerve is severed."[24]

Does it matter that the patient is unaware of this harmful state? In other circumstances, we recognize that harm is done even if the victim is unaware of it. An elderly widow surreptitiously drained of her life savings by an unscrupulous lawyer is the victim of a harmful act whether or not she recognizes it. Selling a child is wrong whether or not the child is capable of protesting. And even though we cannot be absolutely certain a permanently unconscious patient is suffering, these patients exist in a worst possible dehumanizing condition; even if they are unaware of that condition, they are enslaved in perpetual motionlessness, emotionlessness, helplessness, unlike any other form of human existence, isolated from every human connection and communication—an exile, whether perceived or not, that is an even more terrible punishment because it is void of context.

If, upon exercising your empathy and imagination, you find this view persuasive, then withdrawing life-supporting treatment from a patient in a permanent vegetative state becomes not merely ethically permissible but an obligatory act of beneficence.

Understand this decision and you understand the concept of medical futility.

REFERENCES

1. Amudsen DW. The physician's obligation to prolong life: A medical duty without classical roots. *Hastings Center Report* (1978) 8(4):23–30.
2. Hippocratic Corpus, The Art. In: Reiser SJ, Dyck AJ, Curran WJ (Eds.) *Ethics in Medicine: Historical Perspectives and Contemporary Concerns.* Cambridge: MIT Press, 1977:6–7.
3. Truog RD, Brett AS, Frader J. The problem with futility. *New England Journal of Medicine* (1992) 326:1560–4.
4. Pellegrino E. Decisions at the end of life—the abuse of the concept of futility. *Practical Bioethics* (2005) 1(3):3–6.
5. Jecker NS, Schneiderman LJ. Futility and rationing. *American Journal of Medicine* (1992) 92:189–96.
6. Schneiderman, L.J, Jecker, N.S. *Wrong Medicine: Doctors, Patients, and Futile Treatment.* Baltimore: Johns Hopkins University Press, 1995.
7. *Council on Ethical and Judicial Affairs. Current Opinions.* Chicago: The Council on Ethical and Judicial Affairs of the American Medical Association, 1989.
8. Schneiderman LJ, Capron AM. How can hospital futility policies contribute to establishing standards of practice? *Cambridge Quarterly of Healthcare Ethics* (2000) 9:524–31.
9. *In re Baby "K,"* 16 F.3d 590 (4th Cir), *cert.denied,* 513 U.S. 825 (1994).
10. *Emergency Medical Treatment and Active Labor Act* (EMTALA), 42 U.S.C.A. #139dd (West 1992).
11. *Bryan v Rectors and Visitors of the University of Virginia,* 95 F.3d 349 (4th Cir. 1996).

12. Kolata G. Court ruling limits rights of patients: Care deemed futile may be withheld. *The New York Times* 1995, Apr 22: 6 (col. 6).

13. Schneiderman LJ, Manning S. The Baby K Case: A Search for the Elusive Standard of Medical Care. *Cambridge Quarterly of Healthcare Ethics* (1997) 6:9–18.

14. Wanzer SH, Adelstein SJ, Cranford MD, et al. The physicians responsibility toward hopelessly ill patients. *New England Journal of Medicine* (1984) 310:955–9.

15. Wanzer SH, Federman DD, Adelstein SJ, et al. The Physician's responsibility toward hopelessly ill patients: A second look. *New England Journal of Medicine* (1989) 320:844–9.

16. Cranford RE. The persistent vegetative state: The medical reality (Getting the facts straight). *Hastings Center Report* (1988) 18: 27–32.

17. Owen AM, Coleman MR, Boly M, Davis MH, Laureys S, Pickard JD. Detecting awareness in the vegetative state. *Science* (2006) 313: 1402.

18. Medical aspects of the persistent vegetative state. I. The Multi-Society Task Force on PVS. *New England Journal of Medicine* (1994) 330: 1499–1508; Medical aspects of the persistent vegetative state. II. The Multi-Society Task Force on PVS. *New England Journal of Medicine* (1994) 330: 1572–9.

19. *The Anatomy of Exile,* Tabori P, & Harrap, London, 1972.

20. *The Human Condition,* Arendt H, New York: Doubleday and Co., 1959: 10 and 23.

21. Aristotle. *Nicomachean Ethics* VIII: ix 3.

22. Shakespeare, W. *Richard II* I:iii.

23. Shakespeare, W. *Romeo & Juliet* III:iii.

24. *The Drowned and the Saved,* Levi P, New York: Summit Books, 1988: 103.

CHAPTER NINE

Beyond Futility
to an Ethic of Care

Now we move beyond medical futility. Two critics of this concept, philosophers Robert Veatch and Carol Spicer, describe an unnamed patient who pleads: "Don't let them give up on me!"[1] The patient was in the terminal stages of AIDS. He was in the ICU, completely dependent on life support, including a mechanical ventilator and intravenous medications to maintain his blood pressure. All his major organ systems were failing. The physicians had run out of curative treatments. They told him they wanted to write a Do Not Attempt to Resuscitate Order (DNAR) when his heart stopped, as inevitably it soon would. The physicians knew from empirical experience and clinical studies that no matter how energetically they shocked the heart and pounded the chest and pumped his lungs with air, the patient would not survive. Their efforts would be medically futile. Rather than helping him, all they would be doing is torturing him. But Veatch and Spicer objected. What right do physicians have to override this patient's plea by invoking medical futility?

This cry poignantly reveals what is missing from the whole concept of medical care. If medical decision making focuses solely on whether to attempt a particular life-saving technology, a patient who is not offered such treatment might reasonably wonder: Does the physician deem me unworthy of further attention and concern? Am I being discarded? Understandably, the patient might respond with a desperate plea to be kept alive at all costs, insisting on any treatment, no matter how unlikely its chance of success or how undesirable the outcome.

This is the way Veatch and Spicer have framed the futility debate, as a conflict between physician and patient (or surrogate) over the right to decide whether a particular life-saving intervention, such as CPR or mechanical ventilation, should or should not be attempted.[2–7] Either that treatment or nothing. Arguments on behalf of physician's authority to determine medical futility tend to emphasize the limits of the physician's obligations in the face of treatment demands.[2,6,8–14] Opposing arguments reflect a number of concerns, but a particular concern is the potential erosion of recent gains in patient autonomy against medical paternalism.[15–21]

But as the physician, Kathy Faber-Langendoen, the philosopher, Nancy S. Jecker, and I have argued, this limited perspective overlooks, both at the bedside and in public commentary, a whole other set of obligations: the physician's duty not only to do one's best to restore health but also to be just as determined to relieve suffering.[22] In other words, physicians have a duty to adhere to what has been called an ethic of care, the ethical duty to redirect efforts from life-saving treatments that are no longer beneficial toward the conscientious pursuit of treatments that are— treatments that maximize comfort and dignity for the patient and the grieving family. At its most expansive, an ethic of care takes in

not only doctor–patient interactions but also doctor–nurse interactions, and considers the important roles of institutional facilities, insurance policies, and public education.

Like medical futility, an ethic of care has a long-standing
and prominent place in the history of medicine,[23–25] summarized
nicely by the 15th-century French adage, "to cure sometimes, to
relieve often, to comfort always."

Not surprisingly, the most clearly articulated description of an
ethic of care can be found in the nursing literature, where it is
defined as a commitment to protecting and enhancing the patient's dignity.[26] Effective caring goes beyond good intentions or
simple kindness and includes psychological, philosophic or religious, and physical components, taking into consideration the
patient's social context and specific goals. These require their own
specific, well-developed skills.[27,28] And whereas nursing has had a
long tradition of caring, only recently has palliative care come to
be accepted by physicians and used in acute-care hospitals, in
designated palliative-care units, and in institutional and home-
based hospice programs.

Critically ill patients tend to face a similar set of treatment decisions at the end of life no matter what the underlying disease.
These include whether or not to attempt CPR if the heart stops,
whether or not to intubate the patient and employ mechanical ventilation if the patient's lungs fail, and whether or not to replace what
the patient cannot eat or drink with tube-provided nutrition and
hydration. Other treatment decisions involve whether or not to employ intravenous drugs to maintain blood pressure or antibiotics
for infections, as well as oxygen, surgery, narcotics, and sedatives.

In my experience, many unnecessary battles are fought over
who has the right to decide whether to withhold or withdraw a

particular life-sustaining treatment. These conflicts tend to dissolve when family members hear physicians present a broader approach to their loved one's treatment, when the discussion includes not only those treatments that will not be attempted because they offer no realistic chance of benefit but those that *will* because they will assure the patient the most comfort. Family members want to hear that their loved ones will be cared for—that the physicians and nurses *care.* Hence, they are more inclined to trust the motives and judgments of physicians when they hear them devoting their attention not simply to the negative act of withholding and withdrawing treatments but also to the positive act of enhancing their loved one's last days of life. Families see that their loved one is not being abandoned because "nothing can be done"—an expression I urge my colleagues never to employ—because there is *always* something physicians can do to assure that the patient is comfortable and free of pain. I remind them that death is inevitable and not necessarily a medical failure. Causing or allowing a *bad* death is a medical failure.

In my view, when the decision has been made to redirect efforts from life prolongation, either because the patient requests it or because life-sustaining treatment is futile, from that moment each intervention should be evaluated according to one standard: *Does it comfort the patient?* In weighing whether to attempt or employ these interventions, it is important to consider the quality of remaining life in terms of pain, dignity, control, function, and emotional and spiritual needs and desires. Therefore, needle punctures, tube feedings, monitors, and other invasive technologies should be avoided unless they clearly contribute to the patient's well-being.

This includes the cardiac monitor, as I discovered on one of my first ethics consultations. I went to the bedside of a woman who was lying there, heavily sedated and dying of cancer. Instead of looking at (and remembering) the woman dying in a blissful sleep, her family was riveted on the cardiac monitor. I saw them groaning and cringing at the agonal gyrations of the dying heart and each convulsive electronic blip. Lest this be the last memory they had of the patient, I immediately went to her physicians and urged them to turn off this unnecessary distraction and allow those at her bedside to redirect their attention to the tranquil image of their loved one dying in her sleep.

A few other principles:

There is no excuse for dying patients to endure unwanted pain. Contrary to the customary statistic bandied about that medicine can alleviate 90% of severe pain, medicine can alleviate *100%* of severe pain. It may require sedating doses of narcotics, but if that is what the patient prefers to pain, that is what the patient should be able to obtain. Physicians should *guarantee* (the word I use) that doses of narcotics, sedatives, or other measures will be provided to completely relieve pain if that is what the patient fears. This is *not* euthanasia. If escalating doses of narcotics are inadequate or if neuro-excitatory side effects occur, such as myoclonus (muscle seizures) or agitated delerium, one can add short-acting benzodiazepines. If this does not produce adequate sedation or if paradoxical agitation occurs, then one can switch to barbiturates such as thiopental, pentobarbital, or phenobarbital while continuing the narcotics.

If the patient no longer wishes to be maintained on a mechanical ventilator or if the treatment is futile, the patient should receive sufficient narcotics *before* removal to eliminate any possibility of respiratory distress (i.e., dying of smothering or drowning), even at the risk of shortening life. Again, this is *not* euthanasia. If the patient is ventilator-dependent for survival, it is likely that the patient will die within a few hours after removal, if not immediately. Thus, arrangements can and should be made in advance to carry this out in a private setting that allows family, loved ones, and friends to say farewell, even in a ceremonial way.

If the patient does not wish to be kept alive by means of tube-feeding or if it is futile, then it is important to reassure family, loved ones, and friends that removing this intervention permits dehydration, which reduces respiratory secretions and the risk of aspiration and death by choking. If patients are allowed to die without artificial food and fluids being forced on them, they enter a state of metabolic acidosis, which can induce a mildly euphoric state of terminal delirium. Persons at the bedside can assist with simple nursing measures like moistening the lips, and thus be involved in keeping the patient comfortable. Unlike the removal of a life-sustaining mechanical ventilator, the time of death is less predictable since it will depend on the patient's illness and condition. It almost always occurs within a week or two. Because of this uncertainty, arrangements should be made, if possible, to move the patient to a private, intimate setting, either at home (with a visiting hospice service) or a hospice residence.

Here is a short list of the essentials of comfort care that I put under the category of "intensive caring." These can involve loved ones, family, friends, spiritual advisers, and hospice.

- Alleviating pain
- Maximizing the patient's control over events
- Allowing for privacy, intimacy, and dignity
- Addressing spiritual needs
- Fostering positive memories for loved ones

As you can see, an ethic of care requires collaborative efforts among health-care professionals. Physicians and nurses have much to learn from each other as well as from experts in hospice care and from researchers who are seeking ways to improve palliative care.[29,30,31]

For example, it was hospice nurses who made the discovery that keeping dying patients well-hydrated with intravenous fluids often adds to patient discomfort by worsening respiratory secretions.[31,32] In days gone by, family members used to gather around the bed of a dying person to hear this person's last uttered words. The belief was that in these last moments, the dying person—who was probably experiencing the euphoria of metabolic acidosis—was being granted an early peek into heaven. Books were printed with collections of their last words.[33] It is one of the terrible ironies of modern medicine that when we scrupulously keep the dying patient hydrated, carefully monitoring and correcting acid-base imbalances, we are robbing that patient of the final blessing nature bestows—a peaceful, tranquilized, *natural* death.

An ethic of care is sometimes seen as coming into force only when cure can no longer be expected, but the French dictum was to comfort *always.* One should be alert to the harms caused by the view of medicine that regards care and cure as diametrically opposed values. Rather they should serve their part in a continuum from a good life to a good death.

Finally, better caring for patients when medical treatment is futile calls for public education and better communication between health professionals and patients. All too often, patients or families demand futile treatment because (as noted in the previous chapter) of the symbolic message such treatment conveys. They

Beyond Futility to an Ethic of Care

have come to feel truly cared for only when the most modern invasive technologies are applied. Images of abandonment are evoked, and words such as "starvation" and "neglect" are used to describe patients who are not connected to intravenous lines, feeding tubes, or ventilators. But as I have already pointed out, futile interventions are poor ways of promoting caring and compassion. Futile treatments actually make a mockery of caring by being substitutes for human communication and touching.

Medicine, like all human enterprises, has its inevitable limits. Although these limits may shift with advances in technology and science, it is deceptive to act as though medicine can conquer all disease, or even death itself. It is not sufficient merely to refrain from offering or using interventions that do not work. Rather, an ethic of care truly means making the best possible decisions, *caring* for patients even when the inevitable limits of the physician's powers to prolong life are reached.

REFERENCES

1. Veatch RM, Spicer CM. Medically futile care: the role of the physician in setting limits. *American Journal of Law & Medicine* (1992) 18: 15–36.
2. Brett AS, McCullough LB. When patients request specific interventions: defining the limits of the physician's obligations. *New England Journal of Medicine* (1986) 315: 1347–51.
3. Blackhall LJ. Must we always use CPR? *New England Journal of Medicine* (1987) 317: 1281–4.
4. Youngner SJ. Who defines futility? *Journal of the American Medical Association* (1988) 260: 2094–5.

5. Youngner SJ. Futility in context. *Journal of the American Medical Association* (1990) 264: 1295–6.

6. Faber-Langendoen K. Resuscitation of patients with metastatic cancer: is transient benefit still futile? *Archives of Internal Medicine* (1991) 151: 235–9.

7. Truog RD, Brett AS, Frader J. The problem with futility. *New England Journal of Medicine* (1992) 326: 1560–4.

8. Tomlinson T, Brady H. Ethics and communication in do-not-resuscitate orders. *New England Journal of Medicine* (1988) 318: 43–6.

9. Miles SH. Informed demand for "non-beneficial" medical treatment. *New England Journal of Medicine* (1991) 325: 512–5.

10. Schneiderman LJ, Spragg RG. Ethical decisions in discontinuing mechanical ventilation. *New England Journal of Medicine* (1988) 318: 984–8.

11. Hackler JC, Hiker FC. Family consent to orders not to resuscitate: reconsidering hospital policy. *Journal of the American Medical Association* (1990) 264: 1281–3.

12. Jecker NS. Knowing when to stop: the limits of medicine. *Hastings Center Report* (1991) 21: 5–8.

13. Schneiderman LJ, Jecker NS, Jonsen AR. Medical futility: Its meaning and ethical implications. *Annals of Internal Medicine* (1990) 1112: 949–54.

14. Tomlinson T, Brody H. Futility and the ethics of communication. *Journal of the American Medical Association* (1990) 264: 1276–80.

15. Lantos JD, Singer PA, Walker RM, et al. The illusion of futility in clinical practice. *American Journal of Medicine* (1989) 87: 81–4.

16. Angel M. The case of Helga Wanglie. *New England Journal of Medicine* (1991) 325 (51): 1–2.

17. Wolf SM. Conflict between doctor and patient. *Law, Medicine & Health Care* (1988) 16: 197–203.

18. Callahan D. Medical futility, medical necessity: the-problem-without-a-name. *Hastings Center Report* (1991) 21: 30–5.

19. Capron AM. In: Wanglie H (Ed.). *Hastings Center Report* (1991) 21: 26–8.

20. Scofield GR. Is consent useful when resuscitation isn't? *Hastings Center Report* (1991) 21: 28–36.

21. Katz J. Abuse of human beings for the sake of science. In: Caplan AL (Ed.). *When Medicine Went Mad.* Totowa, NJ: Humana Press, 1992: 233–70.

22. Schneiderman LJ, Faber-Langendoen K, Jecker NS. Beyond futility to an ethic of care. *American Journal of Medicine* (1994) 96:110–4 and *American Journal of Medicine* (1995) 99:443–4.

23. Hauerwas S. Care. In: Reich WT (Ed.) *Encyclopedia of Bioethics.* Vol 1. New York: Free Press, 1978: 145–50.

24. Nelson AR. Humanism and the art of medicine: our commitment to care. *Journal of the American Medical Association* (1989) 262: 1228–30.

25. Jecker NS, Self JD. Separating care and cure: an analysis of historical and contemporary images of nursing and medicine. *Journal of Medicine & Philosophy* (1991) 16: 285–306.

26. Gadow SA. Nurse and patient: the caring relationship. In: Bishop A, Scudder J (Eds.). *Caring, Curing, Coping: Nurse, Physician, Patient Relationships.* Birmingham: University of Alabama Press, 1985: 31–43.

27. Ray MA. Technological caring: a new model in critical care. *Dimensions in Critical Care Nursing* (1987) 6: 166–73.

28. Cooper MC. Principle-oriented ethics and the ethic of care: a creative tension. *Advances in Nursing Science* (1991) 14: 22–31.

29. Coyle N. Continuity of care for the cancer patient with chronic pain. *Cancer* (1989) 63: 2289–93.

30. Walsh TD. Continuing care in a medical center: the Cleveland Clinic Foundation Palliative Care Service. *Journal of Pain & Symptom Management* (1990) 5: 273–8.

31. Printz LA. Terminal dehydration, a compassionate treatment. *Archives of Internal Medicine* (1992) 152: 697–700.

32. Schmitz P, O'Brien M. Observations on nutrition and hydration in dying cancer patients. In: Lynn J (Ed.) *By No Extraordinary Means.* Bloomington: Indiana University Press, 1986: 29–38.
33. Cather, W. *Death Comes to the Archbishop*, New York: Alfred A. Knopf, 1951: 170.

CHAPTER TEN

Future Choices We May All Have to Make

Up to now, we have focused on how to make the best possible medical decisions for a single patient. We have already seen, though, that physicians and loved ones can't always do what they think is best for the patient; they have to take into account a variety of complicating, so-called "external factors." These include whether the definitive treatment is available, such as a compatible organ for transplantation; whether the patient can afford or has health insurance coverage for the treatment; whether the proposed treatment is in accord with the patient's social, cultural, or religious beliefs; and whether those beliefs cause the patient to reject a beneficial treatment or demand a futile treatment. Because of people's increasing expectations for miracles and the enduring complexity of human nature and social forces, these matters will continue to disturb us for a long time. And because, even as we develop more sophisticated and successful—and costly—technology and medications, we still will not cure death in the foreseeable future.

In this concluding chapter I will focus on two large areas of difficult choices we probably will all have to make in this age of "miracles."

One: *We will have to acknowledge the inevitable necessity of rationing health care along with the inescapable duty to provide universal health care.* This means reconciling respect for individual choice (and its potential for infinite demands, including "miracles") with the fair distribution of benefits and burdens that characterize a just society.

Two: *We will have to deal with the public's infatuation with alternative medicine and all its false promises (including "miracles").* In my view, this is a movement that undermines many seriously ill patients and their families, who are lured into dubious and harmful practices.

Notice that I say nothing about the future impact of stem cell research, a "hot topic" that is in the forefront of public controversy today. As I write, opponents who defend the sanctity of life inherent in a microscopic cluster of embryonic cells are exchanging outraged speeches and statements and statutes with proponents who hope to benefit from future life-saving treatments. At the risk of violating Yogi Berra's Law ("Prediction is very hard, especially when it's about the future."), I predict that this fiery exchange will disappear the moment one or more life-saving treatments result from this research—which, alas, will not be as soon as many hope. Today, those who proclaim the "sanctity of life" object to seeking and fashioning treatments that require destroying these microscopic cells. But what if this research leads to a life-saving treatment of insulin-dependent diabetes mellitus?[1] I cannot imagine many "sanctity-of-life" parents denying this treatment to their young severely ill daughter suffering from diabetes. In my view, emotions, passions, family love, ethical argument, and, if necessary, even the law (which overrules Christian Scientist and Jehovah's Witness parents when they try to prevent their children from receiving life-saving treatments) will unite conclusively on the side of saving the life of the young girl, and moral arguments on behalf of the cluster of early embryonic cells will lose their weight and fly away—like airplanes that also were once opposed for religious reasons.

RATIONING AND UNIVERSAL HEALTH CARE

Let us start with a patient I will call Ernesto. He was a handsome 25-year-old Mexican, with flashing dark hair and piercing dark eyes. Unfortunately, he also possessed a failing heart that so incapacitated him he could not get out of bed. Even more unfortunate, he was born on the south side of the Mexican–American border. His family had loaded him in their car and rushed him to our hospital across this border just in time for him to be rescued in the Emergency Department. His diagnosis was severe idiopathic cardiomyopathy—massive destruction of his heart muscles, possibly due to a recent undetected viral illness—with end-stage congestive heart failure.

Barely conscious, he was placed on continuous intravenous medication designed to keep up his blood pressure in hopes that he might gradually improve. This went on for over a month with no end in sight. Every time an attempt was made to wean him from his intravenous medications, he went into shock. His ever-present family of father, mother, brothers and sisters, cousins, aunts and uncles who filled the room made a worshipful scene that could have been painted on the ceiling of the Sistine Chapel. They knew the American doctors would not let their beautiful Ernesto die.

As far as the doctors were concerned, their best hope was to discharge Ernesto back to his home in Mexico. But this was proving to be impossible. There was no likelihood he could be kept alive at home, and it was very likely he would die during transportation. So there he was, in the ICU, where it looked as though he would require intensive hospital care indefinitely.

"What should we do now?" That's when I was called in as an ethics consultant. Because he was otherwise young and healthy, the optimal treatment—indeed, the standard treatment for this young man in any first-world country—would have been a heart transplant. But this was out of the question. Even though he was *in* a first-world country, Ernesto did not have the means to pay for the procedure.

Social services looked about for state or federal funding and scoured the community for private sources, but they were unsuccessful. No surprise. In addition to the initial expense of the heart transplant—not to mention the problem of providing a scarce organ to someone who wasn't even a U. S. citizen—there would be the costs and burdens of long-term follow-up care, including multiple medications and periodic across-the-border check-ups as long as he lived. (Sometimes medical advances do away with ethical dilemmas but not in this case. Although mechanical left ventricular assist devices have been developed since then as an alternative to heart transplants, the follow-up difficulties would have been just as insurmountable.)

As you can imagine, the young residents bonded very closely with Ernesto. We brainstormed many therapeutic options, including several that were admittedly "off-the-wall," such as attempting to gain him citizenship, either by petitioning for a special act of Congress or by marrying him to one of the women caring for him. We didn't want to overlook anything.

Naturally, we also had to discuss more realistic, albeit much less appealing, options, including keeping him comfortable until he either revived miraculously or died of an inevitable cardiac arrest. Or, inform his family that we would continue ICU treatment for a limited time only. In the end, the physicians waited until Ernesto's heart finally gave out, and then, unable to face the eager and imploring family without "doing something," they performed a "Hollywood code," a term that arose in medical circles out of sheer exasperation. A "Hollywood code" is attempted CPR that physicians know will be ineffective but they do anyway—for show. It is a piece of theater enacted when the demand is made on them to perform CPR on a patient they know will not recover. Physicians do it when they are unable to persuade family members of the procedure's futility and don't want to spend any more time trying. They just go through the motions, perhaps a bit dramatically as in the movies or on television. Although roundly condemned by medical ethicists (including me), I had to accept that this bit of deception in this particular case seemed to be the best possible medical treatment. The family was plunged in grief, but they embraced the physicians, weeping, with the solace that "they had done everything."

Ernesto could not receive a heart transplant because he lacked the proper credentials of citizenship. Was that just? The way the world works in defining national borders, I'm afraid so. The simplest definition of justice is the fair distribution of burdens and benefits within a society. Ernesto, a non-citizen who lived in Mexico, did not share the burdens of citizenship, such as income taxes, possible military obligation, and so forth, that would justify his obtaining U. S. benefits. But would being an American citizen have been enough?

Here is the story of another patient. In 1992 the public was outraged by news reports that a felon in a California prison for armed robbery received a heart transplant at the Stanford Medical Center. (His name was never released to the public.) The airwaves and newspapers clamored at the injustice. Commentators railed indignantly that an anonymous prisoner could get a heart transplant, but their hardworking, law-abiding friends and relatives could not. Why? Because, unlike the prisoner, whose treatment was paid for by the government, they lacked the right kind of health insurance.

In fact, another transplant candidate, a 55-year-old man named Mike Miraglia (his real name), who shared an ICU room at Stanford University Medical Center for 8 days with the prisoner and his two guards, was passed over in favor of the prisoner. He also had been considered a good match for the donor heart but was still recuperating from earlier surgery when the heart became available.

Ironically, Mr. Miraglia did not seem to share the public outrage. He even sent a get-well card to the prisoner, with the message that perhaps the inmate's new heart heralded the beginning of a new life. (Alas, it didn't. He died in prison shortly thereafter amid controversy over whether it was his neglect or the prison's neglect that caused his death.)

The rest of the public, or at least those who vented their wrath, were not so saintly. They could not understand, at a time when so many people were forced to go without basic health care, how an incarcerated criminal could receive a medical treatment that was estimated to cost in the range of $150,000 to $200,000. And that was just the for the surgery; follow-up medications would cost as much as $21,000 per year. Indeed, Department of Correction officials at the time estimated that total costs, including security costs, could amount to $1 million before the inmate was released.

All this because the U.S. Supreme Court had already ruled that "deliberate indifference" to a prison inmate's health problems violated the U. S. Constitution's Eighth Amendment prohibition against "cruel and unusual punishment." Not to mention that international human rights organizations such as Amnesty International cited the 1979 Oath of Athens for Prison Health Professionals, in which adherents pledge "to provide the best possible health care for those who are incarcerated in prisons for whatever reasons, without prejudice."

As the official spokesman for the California Department of Corrections told the *Sacramento Bee:* "We have a requirement, based in law and in losing many, many lawsuits, to provide medically necessary care to inmates. The courts have told us that inmates have a constitutional right to healthcare. You and I don't, but inmates do. . . . We have to do whatever is medically necessary to save an inmate's life. . . . "

In my own 10 minutes of fame (Andy Warhol owes me 5 more) I was interviewed about this case on television's popular news program "60 Minutes" and tried to redirect the public's anger: "Don't blame the docs who are doing the heart transplant," I pleaded. "Blame ourselves and our politicians who have made such a hodgepodge and patchwork of health care insurance in this country."

There was a reason I wanted to redirect the public's wrath. At the time the criminal received the heart transplant there were probably hundreds, maybe even thousands, of patients in the surrounding area who could have used the heart. (Along with cancer, heart disease is one of the top causes of morbidity and death.) All they lacked was health insurance coverage. Why? Because unlike the rest of the first-world countries, the United States fails to provide universal health insurance. If these citizens had the means to pay for the heart transplant, any one of them would have benefited more from the procedure simply by being able to function actively in the outside world. All other factors being equal, including organ compatibility and clinical urgency, as a matter of medical justice, their level of benefit would have placed the person higher on the priority list than someone limited to the confines of a prison.

It is worth spending a little time exploring the issues of *medical justice* and *societal justice* brought to light by these dramatic and infuriating cases.[2]

In an episode from his autobiography, Hans Zinsser, who later became a famous infectious disease expert, described the efforts expended in the early twentieth century to rescue a dying patient named Konig, who strangled a woman to death, then stabbed himself in the abdomen with a bread knife.[3]

Although no one doubted that the "blond and stocky ruffian" was a brutal murderer, an eminent surgeon rapidly mobilized his team of expert assistants and saved the man's life. After 3 months of hospital convalescence, Konig recovered, was duly put on trial, found guilty, and electrocuted. Zinsser, a medical intern at the time, took a dim view of what he regarded as wasted effort, but the response of the doctors was clearly in keeping with the time-honored tradition of *medical justice.*

As a profession, physicians owe (even if they do not always uphold) the ideal of service to anyone in need who can benefit from medical treatments—even murderers—without regard to ethnic, racial, societal, or economic factors. And although this ideal may be compromised when physicians face resource limitations, such as ICU bed shortages, I believe that the ideal nevertheless remains.

The medical ethicist, Haavi Morreim, adds a modification that in this era of soaring medical costs, physicians are duty-bound to exercise responsible stewardship over medical resources.[4] Indeed, economists predict that at least over the next decade national health spending will continue to grow faster than the nation's Gross Domestic Product.[5] The United States spends almost twice as much per capita for health care than other modern countries that provide universal coverage. Unlike these other countries, the United States fails to provide health insurance for over 40 million people (about 17%).[6,6a] Morreim contends that it is simply unrealistic to suppose that physicians can wait until society's allocation scheme is just before they begin to participate in serious cost containment. "[W]hile he cannot assure that resources saved in one instance will be devoted to other needier patients, the physician nevertheless can be sure in a negative sense that whatever he spends on one patient will *not* be available to others. . . . Thus the physician cannot escape a direct role [in rationing medical care].[7]

Granting this qualification, the philosopher Nancy S. Jecker and I emphasize that the *primary* obligation of physicians still must be to act in the best interests of their patients. In fact, whenever physicians have violated this obligation—for example, when evidence appeared that their actions were affected by financial self-interest, such as ownership of laboratory or X-ray facilities or connections with drug companies—the medical profession as well as the lay public rose up in condemnation.[8,8a,8b,8c,8d,8e] As citizens in society, physicians can and should contribute to social health policy decisions. But when they are at the bedside of an individual patient, they should avoid making unilateral rationing decisions.

There is a reason for this. In our open system of health care, there is no guarantee that a rationing decision made by a physician at the bedside of one patient will follow the same standard as a rationing decision made by another physician at the bedside of another patient. There is no mechanism to assure fairness, no over-arching rule for all. One physician might consider $100,000 too much to pay to continue the treatment on the first patient, whose prognosis might actually be better than that of the second patient whose physician might not consider $500,000 too much and continue with an even more expensive treatment.

In contrast to the longstanding tradition of medical justice, *societal justice* first gained public attention in the 1960s, when renal dialysis became available to a limited number of patients as a life-saving treatment. Physicians recognized that many patients were potential beneficiaries of this new treatment and that unprecedented choices had to be made. To help make these choices, physicians enlisted the formal assistance of lay committees, as representatives of society—soon disparaged as "God Squads." Although this process was roundly condemned, it is probably more accurate to call it the first attempt to confront society with the distressing reality of rationing. Notions of medical justice (some patients will benefit more than others) and societal justice (choices inevitably have to be made) were unfamiliar to those early participants.[9] As I have already noted, to our continuing distress, American society and politicians still cannot honestly face these issues. But we will have to.

In a just society, principles of distributive justice govern the distribution of burdens and benefits. In every community composed of individuals of varying ages, fortunes, skills, talents, capacities, strengths, and weaknesses, morally arbitrary apportionment of burdens and benefits will occur unless deliberate redistributive mechanisms are put in place.

Which brings us to the question of whether a criminal is entitled to a heart transplant just like any other member of society, as has been decreed by the U.S. Supreme Court. Jecker and I argue that if society considers the criminal to be a full member of a just society, then that person would be entitled to at least a "decent minimum"—namely, that level of care considered basic to all members of that society. The question would then follow: Does that level of health care include equal access to beneficial heart transplants? Probably not—as long as available hearts are as limited as they are today.

But even if criminals are not considered entitled to the same level of medical care afforded all members of a society, that does not mean they are not entitled to receive any medical care at all. There is actually a lower level of care, a kind of "rudimentary decent minimum" granted to persons on simple humanitarian grounds—namely, emergency treatments given to anyone entering an emergency department, even if they are not considered members of our society, including illegal immigrants such as Ernesto. Does that "rudimentary decent minimum" include access to heart transplants? Almost certainly not.

Throughout this chapter, and indeed in many places in the book, I have referred to terms like justice and "decent minimum," and I have alluded to the *in*justice resulting from of our lack of universal health care in the United States. Now I shall try to present ways in which we can approach the notion of justice and give a practical, working definition of a "decent minimum" of health care that is an essential component of justice.

The simplest definition of justice is the fair distribution of burdens and benefits. A just society seeks to implement this principle for all its citizens. Within *spheres* of justice is an array of *resources,* such as money, honors, food, shelter, health care, welfare, and education, that a just society would attempt to distribute justly.[10]

Within *fields* of justice is an array of *criteria,* such as urgency of need, capacity to benefit, value to society, future potential, and past services rendered, that a just society would consider in distributing a scarce resource.[11] How can we proceed from these generalities to the specifics of health-care justice?

In his book, *A Theory of Justice,*[12] the philosopher John Rawls proposes a thought experiment that gives us a good place to start. He asks us to imagine behind a "veil of ignorance—that is, before we are born—what kind of society we would want to enter. We would not know anything about the strengths and weaknesses we would bring into the world. We would not know, for example, whether we would be rich or poor, highly intelligent and strong, endowed with a sturdy constitution or predisposed to life-long illness, or severely disabled, mentally or physically.

What kind of society would we want to enter? Wouldn't we want a society that enables us to live as best as reasonably possible, no matter what our capacities or limitations? If we were lucky enough to be healthy, strong and gifted physically or mentally, we would want to have the opportunity to exercise these capacities, prosper, and be successful. But if we were not so lucky and were dependent on others to make use of our limited capacities, we would want those who were more fortunate to help us.

Therefore, we would want society to distinguish between what is *unfortunate* and what is *unfair*.[13] When illness strikes, it is *unfortunate.* (Simply look around: despite our worthy efforts to make people feel responsible for their own state of health, cancer and drunken drivers strike the slim and fit as well as the overweight and slothful.) We would regard a society that fails to take responsibility for assisting a citizen in recovering from this misfortune as *unfair.* In other words, we would consider health care an obligation of a just society—a fundamental matter of fairness.

As Norman Daniels stated, "[h]ealth care is of special moral importance because it helps to preserve our status as fully functioning citizens."[14] Or, as noted by H. Zollner, "Equity should be everybody's concern, because inequities in health are everybody's loss. They harm many people, operate on a socioeconomic gradient, and put a strain on economic development and social cohesion."[15]

Unlike most European countries, the United States does not seem to recognize health care as a matter of both ethics and economics. How does one account for this difference? Despite contrasts drawn by social critics who emphasize traditions of North American capitalism versus European socialism, there is great similarity in the values shared by all liberal democracies: politically, there is respect for individual rights and the rule of law; economically, a belief in a free market and free enterprise to maximize society's material benefits. At the same time, all these societies—including the United States—recognize that restraints must be imposed on economic freedom to "eliminate or compensate for natural variations or for the contingencies of social life."[16]

At the present time no European country attempts to support its citizens with a totally regulated centralized economy. Nor has the United States, despite its trumpeted allegiance to capitalism, ever had a totally unregulated free market economy. All these countries recognize that to safeguard a liberal democracy, to maintain what in Europe is called "solidarity," it is necessary to actively redistribute material goods from the more fortunate to the less fortunate.

Why has the United States failed to apply this notion to health care? Exploring this question and examining the problems encountered by the United States in addressing what most European nations consider an essential obligation of a just society gives us an opportunity to radically examine the notion of justice itself.

We shall have to look to history and culture as well as the economic and political systems for answers. Quite obviously, the North American and European continents have had vastly different historical experiences. In contrast with Europeans' collective memories of centuries of devastating wars, famines, and brutal religious and class conflicts, North Americans bask in a more cheery self-image of rugged individualism, best symbolized by the solitary, heroic American cowboy, who in reality rode the plains only briefly yet has continued to ride the plains for over a century in mythology. Along with this self-image is a distrust of a centralized bureaucracy (especially since it usually demands the cowboy's tax support) and a preference for private enterprise as opposed to government entitlements, even to the point of believing in the free-market approach to addressing all sorts of social needs—including health care.

Many Americans conceive of justice in a way that is peculiarly American. To them justice exists in the lavish and widespread wealth and high standard of living (ignoring the ever-widening gap between the very rich and the rest of the population), that have been achieved by calling forth each person's best efforts and allowing the benefits of these efforts to be distributed in a (theoretically) unfettered way. The material success of capitalism has confirmed the beliefs of the true believers. Small wonder that these true believers—and there are many—view with suspicion, if not alarm, any hand other than the Unseen Hand that "unjustly" tries to alter this state of affairs.

The American economist Henry Aaron dourly summarized the above perspective:

> "The U.S. health care administration, weird though it may be, exists for fundamental reasons, including a pervasive popular distrust of centralized authority, a federalist governmental structure, insistence on individual choice (even when, as it appears to me, choice sometimes yields no demonstrable benefit), the continuing and unabated power of large economic interest, and the virtual impossibility (during normal times in a democracy whose Constitution potentiates the power of dissenting minorities) of radically restructuring the nation's largest industry—an industry as big as the entire economy of France."[17]

Two other features of U. S. society have interfered with achieving universal health care. Far more than European countries, the United States is inhabited by people who have immigrated from many different parts of the world. They constitute many different religions, ethnic groups, and races. Unlike the more homogeneous societies of Europe—particularly Scandinavian countries whose citizens tend to share such similar physical and cultural traits they could almost be (and, more than Americans, are) blood relatives— many Americans have difficulty feeling empathy for other, very

161

different Americans. They don't easily embrace the concept of solidarity. Although this indifference is distressing, it may prove not to be a failing unique to the United States now that solidarity is being severely tested in European countries that are experiencing their own waves of immigrants and rising health-care costs. Indeed, it will be interesting to see which comes first: achievement of an all-inclusive universal health care by the United States or the abandonment of the principle of all-inclusive solidarity in Europe.

Another feature of U. S. society that has interfered with achieving universal health care is a toxic side effect of the belief in the superiority of the free market as a solution for social problems— powerful, self-interested, profit-oriented health-care institutions. This will be a risk for European countries that are beginning to look at this approach as a way to deal with their own mounting health-care costs.

How effective is the market- and profit-oriented approach to providing a just health-care system? In the United States, this notion was given its most expansive test during the 1970s and 1980s under the rubric Managed Competition. The idea was to encourage large health-care institutions to compete with each other for the health-care dollar of consumers under limited guidelines intended only to keep the process on track. Consumers (or their representatives) were expected to choose what they considered the best health-care plans based on quality and price. Competition was expected to favor the most desirable health-care plans, weed out the less desirable ones and, most important, reduce health-care costs. The underlying premise was that choosing a health-care plan was no different than choosing a car. Products of varying value and price would be presented to the informed consumer who would choose at a preferred intersection of these two variables—just like choosing between a Chevy and a Porsche.

Many problems soon became apparent, some readily predictable:

- Patients rarely are as capable of making informed choices about their future health-care needs as they are about a car. This is so whether they are healthy and unable to imagine what they will require when they become sick or if they are forced to choose under the stress of an active illness. Many patients discovered too late that the cheap health-care plan they had chosen did not cover treatments they later needed.

- In some instances, patients, unwilling to accept any cost trade-off, sued to receive the more expensive treatments, and the courts agreed, thus undermining an important element of cost control. For example, patients went to court to obtain costly bone marrow transplantation for metastatic breast cancer—whose value had not been established and in fact was later disproved—and the courts, moved more by the pleas of desperately ill patients than by the cold calculations of medical evidence, forced health-care plans to ignore contract limitations and cover the costs.

- Health care does not fit into the standard notion of production and consumption. In the usual business transaction the producer offers and the consumer chooses. In medicine, the physician makes the diagnosis and determines the treatment, hence, in every important respect, controls both production and consumption.

- As health-care plans struggle to control costs, they engage in various strategies of risk selection ("cherry picking"), seeking the healthy and avoiding the sick, especially the really sick.
- For-profit health-care plans have a conflict of fiduciary obligation, often focusing on raising the value of their stocks to please their shareholders at the expense of serving their patients.
- A paradox emerged that separated health care from the usual market model. Whereas a traditional business increases productivity and efficiency as it improves its procedures over time, just the opposite occurs in medicine. As medicine improves its procedures, it produces more survivors of once-fatal illnesses, hence creates a negative feedback by plugging the system with more elderly, disabled, and chronically ill.

As you can see, the struggle over health care in the United States has led to experiences that may soon plague those countries that already have universal health care but are undergoing similar strains on the system due to social, technological, and economic changes.

From these experiences arise certain inescapable questions:

- Can policymakers reconcile the obligations of society to all its citizens (universality) with allowing freedom of choice (individualism)?
- Can policymakers reconcile the inevitable necessity of health-care rationing with the rising expectations of citizens in a liberal democracy?

One experiment in the state of Oregon attempted to do what no other state or even country has done—namely, openly seek citizen input in determining health-care treatment priorities. In other words, given the opportunity to express their opinions, which treatments did the people want more than others? The experiment was directed at improving the range of options for those patients who were dependent on state-funded welfare and had the most difficulty affording health care.

Through a series of community meetings an Oregon Health Plan was devised that aggregated individual preferences and placed conditions and treatments in a hierarchy, depending on the expressed preferences of those who took (and had) the time to participate in these community meetings. It was agreed that all treatments that could be funded within the state's budgetary limit would be insured, and all those that fell outside the limit would not. This is rationing—openly directed by the people themselves. Although the process met with considerable criticism and controversy (including its limitation to poor patients on welfare), one certain benefit was that by granting priority to the most cost-beneficial treatments and eliminating marginally or rarely beneficial treatments that were very expensive, the roster of qualified patients could be enlarged and the range of useful treatments could be expanded.

One conceptual flaw, however, was that the cost–benefit analyses were aimed only at the cost to society and the benefit to the individual. Benefit to society was not considered. As a result, an important consideration was neglected—the interdependence between the individual and society. Justice, you recall, is the fair distribution of *both* benefits and burdens. In this case, the fact that individualism cannot survive without the support of the community was overlooked—an unfortunate characterization of many American choices.

One of the most serious problems in the pursuit of a just health-care system is that politicians and policymakers have become transfixed by the fear of soaring health-care costs. Despite compelling evidence that single-payer universal health care is more economical, acceptable and effective than all the alternatives, politicians and policymakers quarrel without let-up over the alternatives. Should Medicare be expanded? Should it be "privatized?" Should the federal government play any role at all? What about the state government? How much should be the responsibility of individuals and how should the tab be presented—via tax credits, payroll deductions, cash co-pays, health savings accounts? How should insurance obligations be divided between employee and employer? Should large corporations be required to offer health insurance? What about small businesses? Or businesses with low-income workers and small profit margins?

In other words, almost everyone is preoccupied with *how* to pay for health care. Hardly any thought is being given to *what* should be paid *for*—as though health care is a commodity that needs no examination with regard to what health outcomes should be achieved in a just society.

As a result, inconsistent—even incoherent—rules, regulations, and statutes squeeze and contort the flow of health-care dollars, and, not surprisingly, squeeze and contort the quality and distribution of health-care services. Some Americans, some of the time, are covered by a variety of health insurance policies, some of them useful, some of them not. Many others—well over 40 million Americans—are not covered at all. They can only envy the puzzling assortment of citizens in special categories who have *guaranteed* health insurance, including members of the military and veterans (okay), those over 65 years old (oh well), people with kidney failure (why just them?), select government workers including members of Congress (huh?), and prisoners (are you kidding!). Health care is not only a mess, it is *unjust.*

Why have these gated communities been constructed? For one simple reason: to control costs.

Are politicians and policymakers right to be transfixed by the inevitability of out-of-control costs under a universal system? Is there an ethical and fiscally responsible solution to the dilemma of providing for individual desires and simultaneously meeting societal responsibilities? As I noted, to answer these questions we need to expand our thinking beyond how to pay for health care to what should be paid *for.* This will require us to make tough choices, but the choices will be based on principles everyone can understand rather than on arbitrary categories.

First of all, with regard to health care, we must accept that everyone is *not* entitled to everything. Everyone *is* entitled to what Norman Daniels calls a fair opportunity—namely, a "decent minimum" level of health care. What is a decent minimum? In my opinion, it is a level of health care that enables a person to acquire an education, hold a job, and raise of family. Or, if the person is unable to meet these goals because of ill health, it is a level of health care that enables a person to attain a reasonable level of function within the person's limits, as well as a reasonable level of comfort, whether it be from pain or other forms of suffering.

This definition recognizes the importance of each person, not in isolation, but in relationship to other members of a just society. And it assures that society's needs for productive citizenry are recognized as a practical trade-off for the burden of health care costs all of us in that society have assumed. To achieve these goals we do away with our preoccupation with lists of treatments that are tallied merely in accordance with procedure charges (which are not the same as costs) and bureaucratic sources of funding but are not connected to health-care *outcomes*. In sociological parlance, health-care decisions will have to be "operationalized," namely specified in terms of health-care treatments that are directed toward achieving the decent minimum goals described above (the latter providing the evidence-based outcome measures) for each *person*. Health care as well as insurance coverage will have to be relevant to each patient's particular needs.

Let's take a particular example, diabetes mellitus, and track it through a person's lifespan. It is a common disease with potentially severe and disabling effects—particularly on the cardiovascular system, the kidneys, and the nervous system—which can be reduced, prevented, or alleviated with optimal treatment. A decent minimum level of health care would start with guaranteed prenatal care to give the developing fetus and newborn the best chance for a healthy beginning. From childhood to adulthood, a decent minimum would guarantee that the person received the latest appropriate genetic screening to determine risk, along with ongoing nutritional and lifestyle counseling to reduce risk factors such as obesity. If, despite these preventive measures, the person developed clinical diabetes, he or she would receive guaranteed health insurance coverage for chronic disease management, including optimal glucose control by diet and medication, along with education and monitoring to prevent infections and organ damage. As long as the person was gaining an education, holding a job, or raising a family, these would be the goals toward which an obligatory decent minimum level of treatments would be directed.

Even if the most severe complications occurred during this time, such as heart failure or kidney failure, the decent minimum would include any necessary life-sustaining intensive care, renal dialysis, and organ transplantation that would enable the person to achieve those goals. Later in life, no matter what the age, when the person was no longer pursuing these goals, the emphasis on decent minimum medical care would shift toward guaranteeing treatments that provide a reasonable level of function within the person's limits, as well as a reasonable level of comfort, whether from pain or other forms of suffering. These goals might include enjoying one's loved ones and friends, being with grandchildren, listening to music, visiting museums, traveling abroad, and so forth. A decent minimum level of health care would aim to achieve these goals—once again, even if the patient developed heart or kidney failure and required an organ transplant. In the latter situation, the problem would not be whether the patient was entitled to an organ transplant, but that in competing for such a limited resource the priority of this patient might not be as high as that of other patients whose benefit might be greater. Finally, near the end of life, if the patient suffered from severe dementia or required ongoing intensive—and expensive—acute hospital care to sustain life, then a decent minimum would no longer include treatments like chronic kidney dialysis or organ transplantation directed at prolonging life but would shift toward optimal comfort care.

After reading all this, you might say: *But, wait, isn't this the United States of America? What's happened to our hallowed respect for freedom of choice? Suppose someone wants more than the decent minimum and is willing to pay for it—and it is not medically futile.*

My answer would be: We should permit it.

Won't there be different levels of health care if we allow this?
Yes.
Isn't this unethical?

In my view, no. For the simple reason that if all citizens have at least sufficient health care, a decent minimum that enables them to participate in society, then inequalities can be ethically justified for those who wish to obtain more expensive and elaborate health care on their own, as long as their privilege does not deny others of their rights.

In the end, all societies have to acknowledge that the rising costs of health care are inevitable. But are they unlimited? Not if we accept that with regard to health care, everyone is *not* entitled to everything. Better health always will be an infinite demand, becoming more and more pronounced as more and more treatments for ailments and conditions once accepted as "normal" are deemed to be serious—albeit curable—medical problems.

This trend was adroitly identified by the social critic Ivan Illich (not to be confused with the Tolstoy character described in the Introduction), who coined the term the "medicalization of life" in the mid-1970s to describe the way modern society expanded the concept of medical morbidity to encompass the vast array of life's dissatisfactions.[18] People who are preoccupied with the ordinary fatigues and aches and pains of living, he said, rarely want to acknowledge that they are unhappy with their jobs or their relationships, or are despondent because they are trapped in stressful, unfulfilling life pursuits, or are experiencing existential despair. They want to hear that they are physically ill. They want to hear that their sadness and fatigue and their aches and their pains are ailments for which medicine must assume responsibility.

ALTERNATIVE MEDICINE
OR ALTERNATIVES TO MEDICINE?

This brings me to my second topic, "alternative medicine." It probably is no coincidence that this phenomenon has arisen in the United States in parallel with the rise of medicalization. It is both striking and paradoxical: At the same time patients are demanding—and benefiting from—more and more high technology as well as the latest scientific discoveries in their medical treatments, they are also being drawn to this alluring counterculture. Surveys suggest that at some time or other 40% of Americans employ unconventional treatments and consult some version of alternative practitioners.[19,19a,19b,19c] Alternative medicine has been called "the largest growth industry in health care today."[20]

Alternative medicine interventions, including acupuncture, chiropractic, homeopathy, and naturopathy, are now offered by health maintenance organizations (HMOs), reimbursed by health insurance plans, and even mandated by states—often in the absence of any reliable evidence of efficacy for the conditions for which they are being prescribed. But as one commentator noted, "HMOs have found that people who utilize such alternatives tend to be healthier than the general run-of-the mill patient and so cost the HMO less. In other words, it is profitable to attract the business of alternative medicine enthusiasts, whether the therapies they receive are truly effective or not."[21]

Many states grant licenses to alternative practitioners, expressly authorize physicians to use alternative treatments, prohibit medical boards from disciplining physicians who use such practices, and mandate insurance coverage. The state of Washington has

171

enacted the broadest legislation. It requires health-plan coverage for "every category of health care provider to provide health services or care for conditions included in the basic health plan services."[22] Although the statute specifically requires that the health service be "cost-effective and clinically efficacious," when insurers attempted to exclude certain unorthodox practitioners on the grounds that they did not meet the carrier's standards for provision of cost-effective and clinically efficacious health services, the state insurance commissioner responded by warning that she would "take all enforcement actions necessary" to override their efforts.[23]

It is important to point out that regardless of the popularity of alternative medicine interventions, enthusiastic claims of their efficacy are, for the most part, seriously out of proportion to supporting empirical data gathered even by advocates. One must look for other reasons to account for their popularity. And although "the medical establishment" is roundly criticized for ignoring or even suppressing evidence of the benefits of alternative medicine, the fact is the voluminous studies cited by proponents of some of the best known treatments were conducted without adequate attention to long-established principles of experimental design.[24]

Even more noteworthy is how often proponents of alternative medicine acknowledge the lack of empirical validation for their practices—indeed express disdain for the whole idea of empirical validation—meanwhile retorting that a great deal of contemporary Western medical practice also lacks empirical validation.[25,25a,25b,25c]

But an important development occurred in the last half-century: the introduction of randomized controlled trials to evaluate new medical treatments. Today, physicians expect claims of therapeutic efficacy to be based not on unsubstantiated theories but on a scientific method that includes randomized assignment of intervention and control subjects, informed consent, clear definitions of interventions and outcome measures, unbiased double-blind data collection, appropriate use of statistical analysis, and confirmation of observations by independent researchers. These are the evidence-based standards of contemporary Western medicine. Those of us who practice medicine in this tradition fret mightily when we lack good data rather than complacently accepting it.

There are many ways to fulfill human needs that we do not call medicine, that do not require empirical validation. In addition to physical and psychological well-being, all of us seek things like love and happiness, spiritual fulfillment, and harmonic balance between labor and leisure. We seek them in many ways— listening to music, praying, working, reading, meditating, hiking in the mountains, being with loved ones and friends. We may enthusiastically recommend a book, or a Mozart piano concerto, or a mountain trail, but we don't feel the need to prove this intervention's general validity. We recognize individual differences in tastes and preferences—what works for me may not work for you. In other words, these are ways we seek the good life, each in our own way, without claiming that they are part of medicine. They are *alternatives* to medicine.

How then did we come to use the term "medicine" to describe practices that even proponents admit cannot be empirically validated? The answer, I think and as I already noted, was given to us by Ivan Illich. "Diagnosed ill-health," said Illich, "is infinitely preferable to any other form of negative label or to no label at all."[17] It relieves people of social and political responsibilities and enables them to cash in on their insurance policies.

And, he added, institutions like medicine have been, to use the contemporary jargon, willing enablers. "Social life becomes a giving and receiving of therapy: medical, psychiatric, pedagogic, or geriatric."[18]

Why is the distinction between "alternative medicine" and "alternatives to medicine" important? It is important because most proponents of alternative medicine do not claim that the things they do are alternatives *to* medicine. Rather, they claim that the things they do *are* medicine, that they not only provide such things as spiritual fulfillment, harmonic balance, and happiness for each of us as individuals, but they also cure specific diseases, such as cancer, heart disease, and AIDS, for all of us. They make the *claims* of medicine but disdain the *standards* of medicine.

What can we say about the validity of these claims? I once paid a visit to the alternative health section of the University of California, San Diego bookstore to see what a few of the most celebrated gurus had to say about AIDS, for example. First I looked in the book *Quantum Healing* by Deepak Chopra, M.D.[26] According to Dr. Chopra, AIDS involves a "distortion in the proper sequence of intelligence" in a person's DNA. Siren-like, the AIDS virus emits a sound that lures the DNA to its destruction.[27] "'Hearing' the virus in its vicinity, the DNA mistakes it for a friendly or compatible sound."[27] This is a believable explanation, says Dr. Chopra, "once one realizes that DNA, which the virus is exploiting, is itself a bundle of vibrations."[27] The treatment? Reshape "the proper sequence of sounds using Ayurveda's primordial sound," which will "guide the disrupted DNA back into line."[27] "Once the sequence of sound is restored," Dr. Chopra assures us, "the tremendous structural rigidity of the DNA should again protect it from future disruptions."[27] To put it mildly, Dr. Chopra proposes a treatment and prevention program for AIDS that has no supporting empirical data.

Next I looked up what Christine Northrup, M.D., had to say about AIDS in her book *Women's Bodies, Women's Wisdom.*[28] Dr. Northrup contends that the AIDS epidemic is "a consequence of a large-scale breakdown in human immunity, resulting from such factors as pollution of the air and water, soil depletion, poor nutrition and generations of sexual repression."[29] Her treatment program is vague, flowery, and ultimately misleading. "Long-term AIDS survivors," she states, "and those who have reversed their HIV status to negative, all have the same things in common: They have chosen to transform their lives and their immune systems to resume the power of nature and love."[29] Contrary to her statement, there has never been a documented case of reversal of HIV status.

Then I looked at *Spontaneous Healing* by Andrew Weil, M.D.[30] Dr. Weil approvingly presents the treatment plan of a patient, Mark M., who disparages AZT: "All the people I know who used it are dead"[31]—a fallacious *post hoc* argument that does not require an M.D. degree to recognize. Mark M. attributes his survival to having "a healthy lifestyle and therapies to support the healing system."[32] These therapies include consuming "a lot of raw garlic," hot chile peppers, organic food, "purified" water, and Chinese herbal remedies.[32] In fact, none of these substances, and specifically no Chinese herbal remedy, has ever been shown to benefit patients with AIDS. On the contrary, at the time Dr. Weil was endorsing this regimen, a highly touted Chinese herbal remedy, Compound Q, which was being imported and sold as a cure for AIDS in underground buyers' clubs, was proving to be highly toxic, producing seizures and death.[33]

It is particularly dismaying to remind you that these authors are immensely popular and influential, even respectable—two have lectured at Harvard Medical School (full disclosure here: this is particularly embarrassing—it's my alma mater), and all three have been featured on public television. Had they tried to put any of those sentences in a refereed mainstream medical publication, they would have been immediately challenged by their peers. What is your evidence for that statement? What is the basis for your conclusions? How can you make those factual assertions in the absence of empirical data? And so forth.

These are the kinds of questions that arise from evidence-based contemporary Western medicine. Whereas much of alternative medicine is sustained only by the authority of theories—preferably exotic, ancient, and magical—the tradition of Western medicine is quite the opposite. Theories are not inviolable altars of worship but points of departure for empirical studies. Theories are constantly being pummeled, reshaped, sometimes buttressed, more often completely demolished by data. Indeed, to cite an aphorism well-known to many a chastened scientist (as told to me by one of my mentors, embellishing Thomas Huxley a bit): The Tragedy of Science is when the Beautiful Damsel of Theory is slain by the Dragon of Fact. (This applies also to clinical medicine, wherein some of our most glamorous supermodel theories like bone marrow transplantation for metastatic breast cancer, hormone replacement therapy for elderly postmenopausal women, and orthopedic scraping of osteoarthritic knees have been slain by the dragon of randomized controlled trials.)

Again, we are not talking about living the good life, we are talking about medicine. Medicine cannot fulfill every human need. Yet, with respect to whatever medicine does take responsibility for, it owes a scrupulous attention to empirical data. If we allow ourselves to be uncritically swept up in the wave of enthusiasm for so-called "alternative medicine," physicians risk misinforming and harming their patients; the rest of us risk being their victims. Yes, we all have needs that are not being served by contemporary Western medicine, but these needs do not include being subjected to bogus tests, claims, and treatments. For the fact is, the most highly touted alternative medical treatments have failed to show conclusively any benefit against medical illness. At best, the reported results of their trials are equivocal or contradictory, and because they range widely, both for and against the treatment's efficacy, they suggest considerable interference by nontreatment factors such as patient-selection biases, lack of blinding, and other confounding factors.[34, 34a-34r]

At this point you might say: "So what. It's a free country. If I am a willing patient who consents to treatment by a willing provider, why can't I do that?" The answer is, the two of you are (pretty much) free to do whatever you want, but not to call it whatever you want. Society, not to mention the dictionary, imposes certain constraints. You cannot claim, for example, that when you consult a tennis instructor to cure your sickly backhand you are obtaining medical care. The tennis instructor might enhance your well-being enormously. Still, neither society nor the dictionary (nor the health insurers) would accept a claim that the tennis instructor was practicing medicine. The domain of medicine is and, therefore, alternative medicine should be, defined by certain goals, principles, actions, scope of practice, measures of outcomes, and standards of evidence.

In response to public demand, Congress in 1992 established an Office for the Study of Unconventional Medical Practices, later renamed the Office of Alternative Medicine and then the Office of Complementary and Alternative Medicine at the National Institutes for Health (NIH). The disdainful attitude of the Congressional Appropriations Committee toward "the conventional medical community as symbolized by NIH" comes across without much subtlety in the language of the Appropriation Bill: "The Committee is not satisfied that the conventional medical community as symbolized by NIH has fully explored the potential that exists in unconventional medical practices. . . . In order to more adequately explore these unconventional medical practices the Committee request that NIH establish within the Office of the Director an office to fully investigate and validate these practices."[35] Note that the term used is "validate" not "evaluate," as though the benefits are a foregone conclusion.

Shortly thereafter, in 1994, following a string of deaths from toxic herbal products that aroused the concern of the Food and Drug Administration (FDA), the dietary supplement industry lobbied Congress to pass legislation with the Orwellian name, the *Dietary Supplement Health and Education Act.* This freed the manufacturers of herbal remedies from the authority of the FDA, allowing companies to make wide-ranging claims and bottle all sorts of dubious mixtures without having to prove efficacy. In view of the industry's identification with alternative medicine, this was ironically accomplished by reclassifying their concoctions as food. Dr. David Kessler, the former head of the FDA, had harsh words for the Act, protesting, "this is not about health and this is not about well-being; this is about money and jumping on a bandwagon."[36]

Almost certainly, this legislation reinforced (and was designed to exploit) the public's perception that contemporary Western medicine is withholding miraculous new treatments from desperate patients simply because the treatments have not gone through the dull routine of clinical testing.[37] This widespread belief is based on a misconception that any new untested treatment is more likely to be beneficial than not. In fact the odds are quite the reverse.

For example, the Pharmaceutical Manufacturers Association estimates that for every 5,000 new drugs that are synthesized, 250 make it to animal studies, 5 make it to human trials, and only 1 gets approved by the FDA.[38] In other words, at each step the vast majority of "promising" new drugs are rejected because they are either useless or harmful.

Clearly then, the medical profession behaves irresponsibly if it leads patients to believe that the chances are better than even that a new untested drug will be beneficial. Even more irresponsibly, in the case of alternative medicine, with the vast array of nonvalidated concoctions, pastes, tinctures, extracts, enemas, hormones, megavitamin cocktails, and animal skeletal parts that make up its pharmacopoeia, the harms are magnified if they detour a patient away from truly beneficial therapies. This was directly demonstrated in a study of over 500 patients with breast cancer. The researchers found that "beliefs in the efficacy of alternative treatments including herbal remedies, over-the-counter medications, chiropractic regimens, and, perhaps most importantly, prayer [contrary to those who proclaim its medical benefit] and a reliance on God," substantially contributed to a delayed diagnosis.[39]

I submit that this New Age movement has a parallel in another romantic fantasy that has captured the public imagination again and again throughout history—namely, the belief in a wondrous New Economy, whose magical elements have ranged from tulips to dot-coms. Not long ago we witnessed the impact on thousands of people who lost life savings and jobs when that latest fantasy collapsed, when people finally realized that the claims and expectations of miraculous dot-com profits were not justified by empirical data. And yet, terrible as this was for many people, the New Economy's disaster did not directly involve their health and lives—in contrast to what is at stake when they contend with the miracles promised by New Age healers. Ironically—and fortunately—we have reason to hope that the consequences of these latter beguilements will not be so catastrophic, since nature is more benevolent than greed: most patients presenting to a health-care provider have a self-limited disease; no matter what is prescribed, the patient recovers—the secret underlying many alternative medicine "cures."

Nevertheless, as I said, not all advocates of alternative medicine dismiss the notion of empirical validation. Some provide long lists of references that they claim "the medical establishment" ignores. But the fact is, the vast majority of studies cited by these advocates not only contradict scientific principles supported by years of empirical observations, they were conducted without adequate attention to long-established principles of experimental design.[40]

Why is this important? Because flawed studies tend to overestimate the benefit of treatment.[41,41a,41b] Any deviation from the "fundamental principles of clinical science" makes the outcomes suspect, particularly if they tend to support the predilections of the investigator.[42] And "pooling large numbers of clinical series will not correct the problem of poor controls, it will only give the appearance of greater confidence, but for the wrong answer."[43]

Unfortunately, pointing out these deficiencies has not persuaded true believers. Dr. Wallace Sampson, the editor of the *Scientific Review of Alternative Medicine,* a peer-reviewed journal devoted to objectively analyzing—and invariably debunking—alternative medicine claims, sees his task as pitting the scientific methods of proof against ideology, science against pseudoscience. But, he admits, it's really a "culture war."[44]

Having uttered all these warnings, I do not mean to suggest that every participant in the romantic fantasy of alternative medicine will fail to live up to its claims. Indeed, not every dot-com company listed on the stock exchange was unprofitable. One problem, however, is that the most current term, "complementary and alternative medicine" (CAM), has become the catch-all phrase encompassing whatever the user of the phrase wishes. Critics have suggested that CAM advocates deliberately beef up their credibility by including respected techniques like massage therapy and physical therapy and various psychosocial interventions that have long been part of mainstream medicine. "We've been doing these things for years," complained Dr. Robert S. Baratz, president of the National Council Against Health Care Fraud. "They do not belong to the CAM movement. But CAM advocates are trying to coopt them and mix them in with a bunch of other things."[45]

Indeed, one does not have to accept chiropractic theory that vertebral misalignment is the fundamental cause of disease[46,46a,46b,46c] to acknowledge that spinal manipulation has been shown to be effective for acute low back pain, although perhaps only marginally better than a less expensive educational intervention.[47] Massage therapy, unencumbered by Rolfing mumbo jumbo, has long been a part of standard treatments to alleviate musculoskeletal pain by a wide range of health-care professionals because it is soothing, safe, and noninvasive.

As for acupuncture, it may well be that sticking needles in patients has beneficial effects, but almost certainly such beneficial effects do not require lengthy training in the elaborate theories of a complex meridian system originating in ancient China.[48,48a] In my view, until we have more evidence of the validity of the underlying theories—other than "texts with 2000 years of authority"[49]—I would urge that every time you are about to use the term "acupuncture," substitute the phrase "sticking needles in the body." It is more precise and avoids submitting oneself to arrogant ideology rather than to more humble empirical data.

It is not a new observation that suggestion can achieve powerful effects. In this country and in Europe, hypnosis (our version of acupuncture, perhaps) has been used successfully for over two centuries in a variety of therapeutic circumstances, including to achieve anesthesia during mastectomies and other forms of major surgery.[50]

An argument can be—and has been—made, of course, that some of alternative medicine's rituals and symbols of healing are simply ways to "harness the placebo effect."[51,51a,51b] But rather than incanting the words "placebo effect," we should address it as another mystery of nature, as a valid—even exciting—area for scientific inquiry. In fact, with regard to acupuncture, one proponent, after reviewing a large number of studies, stated that there is "a substantial body of data showing that acupuncture in the laboratory has measurable and replicable physiologic effects that can begin to offer plausible mechanisms for the presumed actions."[52] Sounds good, doesn't it? Yet, in the very same review, apparently unaware of the implications of his statement, he mentions one of the "problems" associated with performing randomized controlled trials: "An inordinately high placebo effect from acupuncture may complicate detection of any intervention-sham difference."[52] In other words, it doesn't seem to matter *where* one sticks the needles.[53,53a,53b]

There are many tantalizing mysteries about placebos. I'll just mention a few. The effectiveness of placebos (substances specifically chosen to be inert and ineffective) varies directly with how dutifully patients in a randomized controlled trial take whatever capsule they have been assigned. In other words, the more placebo pills the patient takes, the more powerful the placebo effect (namely, relief of the symptoms under study). Also, the placebo effect is enhanced if either the patient or prescribing physician has a positive expectation of the capsule—again, no matter what's inside the capsule—and it is enhanced when there are positive interactions between the patient and the physician.[54] And here's another puzzle: Over the last several years the placebo effect in randomized controlled trials of treatment for depression has grown more powerful.[55]

One objection to the scientific methodology underlying contemporary Western medicine often made by proponents of alternative medicine is that in this New Age, patients are held to be so unique that no conclusions can be drawn from randomized controlled trials. A randomized controlled trial, they argue, cannot tell us that a particular patient will not benefit from homeopathy just because it did not work on 100 other patients. There is a legitimate way to respond to this question. It is called the N of one trial—where the patient is his own control.

I once had a patient (I'll call him Leonard), a middle-aged professor, who had just married a younger woman. He began to be concerned about his sexual adequacy and asked me to give him testosterone (this was before the Age of Viagra). From my examination, I regarded Leonard as healthy in all respects and even found that his testosterone level was normal. I was unable to convince him, however, that he was not suffering from testosterone deficiency. So I proposed a trial: For 6 months I would inject him with either testosterone or saline—he would not know which. We would both keep a record and at the end of 6 months we would see what the results were. Every month Leonard came in, I filled a syringe with either testosterone or saline and gave it to the nurse, who injected him without knowing the contents. As we agreed, I kept a record of the treatment given and he kept a record of his sex life. When we sat down and talked at the end of the 6 months, he was persuaded by the results that the testosterone made no difference whatsoever.

To me, that was an honest use of the placebo effect in a way to help Leonard recognize what was really going on, and it led us to a far more fruitful approach to his concerns. An N of 1 trial can be used by anyone who objects to performing a randomized controlled trial on large numbers of patients yet seriously wants to examine whether a treatment effect is specific or a placebo. It meets the standard of informed consent while at the same time testing efficacy in a way that contemporary Western medicine demands.

It is important to remember that medicine is supposed to be a moral profession, and therefore, its practice should withstand popular and economic pressures.[56] We should all be concerned when health-care leaders, policymakers, politicians—and alas, even physicians and medical educators—use as their guiding principle not the search for good empirical data but rather "what the people want" or what people (or insurance companies) are willing to pay for. Not that I think that "what the people want" should be ignored. But, in my view, the proper relationship between society and science is this: Through various political mechanisms, public opinion expresses its concerns and priorities. For example, society has implored scientists to "Find a way to cure and prevent AIDS as soon as possible!" Science is responding and making remarkable progress. However, at every step, determining the most promising research strategy and deciding whether the disease has been conquered and the virus eliminated are not matters of popular opinion but of scientific and medical expertise. Although the contemporary Western medical establishment often is accused of exploiting its power, it is quite striking to me how much power the alternative medicine establishment has wielded throughout the country with so little demonstration of efficacy.

Again, this is not to deny that alternative medicine is fulfilling important emotional needs of patients. Indeed, we all owe it to ourselves to seek explanations other than efficacy against disease to account for its popularity.

Thirty years ago, Robert Avina, a University of California, San Diego medical student collaborating with me interviewed 100 persons in the San Francisco Bay area who were consulting homeopathic practitioners.[57] Why, we wondered, were they seeking medical help from a system that was devoid of any respectable empirical or scientific justification? Were they unsophisticated people who were unaware of modern medicine? On the contrary, we found them to be highly educated patients who were afflicted with chronic diseases with fluctuating courses—diseases that did not cure easily, such as chronic asthma and chronic arthritis. Their perceived needs lay beyond the technology of medicine (which did not give them the cure they were hoping for).

Our interviews taught us something important. Again and again, the patients emphasized that homeopathic practitioners would spend a great deal of time with them, going over their symptoms in meticulous detail before prescribing their treatment, all the while reinforcing that each person was a singular individual.

This is in contrast to contemporary Western medicine, which seeks to classify (and therefore lump) individuals within diagnostic categories. It became apparent to us that these people, who were suffering from incurable illnesses (that remained uncured), were nevertheless made to feel better by practitioners who paid them such intense individual attention. Important emotional needs were being fulfilled—deeply human needs—by their homeopathic practitioners that were being neglected by science-based medicine. Were these practitioners (who probably would not acknowledge it) merely "harnessing the placebo effect"?

One could also argue that for these patients (who probably would not acknowledge it either), the homeopathic practitioners were behaving very much like practitioners of a contemporary Western medical specialty—psychiatry—which is dedicated to addressing emotional needs and which admittedly has tolerated unsubstantiated theories and dubious healers. Indeed, managed care organizations have been particularly intent on calling this specialty to account in terms of cost-effectiveness. Psychiatrists are being penalized for spending far too much time with their patients. This scrutiny is all the more ironic since contemporary Western medical practice, which can now lay claim to demonstrable efficacy in the treatment of many severe emotional disorders, finds itself facing restrictions by the same managed care organizations that are opening their arms to alternative medical practices that have demonstrated no such efficacy.

One thing we have to recognize is that within the next few decades more than half the people living in the United States will be of nonwhite ethnic background. For many of these patients, unconventional therapies will have been handed down over many generations as part of religious or cultural practices or as traditions that arose out of coping with economic privation and lack of access to conventional medical care. Physicians cannot avoid these realities as they seek to provide the best possible treatments to their patients. Nevertheless, if the physician learns that the patient is taking an unconventional treatment, such as a toxic herb[58] that presents a serious hazard to the patient's health, in my view the physician should not hesitate to recommend strongly against the treatment. Respect for multiculturalism should not be used as a sentimental excuse to abandon one's professional obligation to serve the patient's best interests. The physician's range of effort can extend from merely providing information (if that suffices) to negotiating and persuading (if that is successful) to seeking legal action (if that is warranted).

If the physician learns that the "treatment" is costly—for example, if it involves a suspiciously large number of elaborate sessions, and is disproportionate to the patient's illness—the physician probably should express reservations, along with guiding the patient toward reliable information. Among the best currently available sources for gaining accurate information about alternative medical practices are the Web site www.quackwatch .com and publications like *The Scientific Review of Alternative Medicine,* and *Alternative Medicine Alert.* An excellent Web site for help in evaluating news stories that report on health topics is Health News Reviews at www.healthnewsreview.org.

On the other hand, if the condition is serious and treatment of little cost—for example, if the patient has terminal cancer and believes in green tea—the physician can easily agree to add whatever benefit this placebo effect offers to all the other components of good end-of-life care, which might also include (in addition to skillful pain-management) prayer, imaging, meditation, music, art, and any number of other alternatives to medicine.

In all these instances, I believe it is important that the physician not reject or abandon the patient. Whatever the patient chooses to do is part of that patient's individuality and should be respected as such. A good physician would not refuse to care for a patient with heart disease or pulmonary disease just because the patient smoked or abandon a patient with diabetes who took too much pleasure in rich deserts.

Finally, one human need we all have to acknowledge is that throughout history human beings have been drawn toward magic and mysticism—and desperate patients toward snake oil and quackery. It is an inescapable part of the human condition. Again, it is particularly ironic that in the modern era when science has replaced religion as a source of (arduously gained) "miracles," New Age healers—while roundly denouncing medicine—seek medicine's cover to make their own miraculous claims respectable. It is not Alternative Religion these practitioners are advertising but Alternative Medicine. Today, as noted earlier, many false messiahs come with M.D. degrees.

This point is worth emphasizing. There can be no doubt that religious belief provides spiritual comfort to many people, allowing them to connect personally through prayer to a transcendently experienced Supreme Being while at the same time offering a pattern and purpose to life's mysteries, pains, and sorrows. Respect for people's religious beliefs—indeed any deeply felt personal belief—is something we treasure in this country. The problem occurs when a personal belief becomes a generalized claim, either a forceful claim—expressed in bloody violence—that one's belief is

The One True Faith or when the belief is asserted as revealed truth exempt from skeptical inquiry (e.g., prayer cures cancer, AIDS is a result of "generations of sexual repression"). It is in the latter area that I believe alternative medicine trespasses. Yes, alternative medical practitioners seem to fulfill deep human needs, but if they do so through unsubstantiated theories and dubious treatments, they risk causing great harms to trusting patients.

Those of us who practice in the tradition of contemporary Western medicine and even those of us who are not physicians who look around at our dysfunctional health-care system must ask ourselves: Are we contributing to those harms? And as we move more and more into a depersonalizing, time-pressured, efficiency-oriented, for-profit corporate-managed care era, are we being so neglectful of the real needs of those who are ill that we are *causing* trusting patients, friends, and loved ones to be lured toward those unsubstantiated theories and dubious treatments? In this Age of "Miracles," this is something all of us, physicians and laypersons, should take seriously.

REFERENCES

1. Hampton T. Stem cells probed as diabetes treatment. *Journal of the American Medical Association* (2006) 296:2785–86.
2. Schneiderman LJ, Jecker NS. Should a criminal receive a heart transplant? Medical justice vs. societal justice. *Theoretical Medicine* (1996) 17:33–44.
3. Zinsser H. *As I Remember Him: The Biography of R.S.* Boston: Little Brown, 1940:149–50.
4. Morreim H. Cost containment: challenging fidelity and justice. *Hastings Center Report* (1988) 18(6):20–25.

5. Heffler S, Smith S, Keehan, S, Borger C, Clemens MK, Truffer C. U.S. Health Spending Projections for 2004–2014. *Health Affairs.* February 23, 2005: (Web Exclusive) WF 74–85.

6. Reinhardt UE, Hussey PS, Anderson GF. U.S. Health Care Spending In An International Context. *Health Affairs* (2004) 23(3):10–25.

6a. Fuchs VR, Emanuel EJ. Health Care Reform: Why? What? When? *Health Affairs* (2005) 24(6):1399–14.

7. Morreim at 23.

8. Mitchell JM, Sunshine JH. Consequences of physicians' ownership of health care facilities—joint ventures in radiation therapy. *New England Journal of Medicine* (1992) 327:1497–501.

8a. Swedlow A, Johnson G, Smithline N, Milstein A. Increased costs and rates of use in the California workers' compensation system as a result of self-referral by physicians; *New England Journal of Medicine* (1992) 327:1502–06

8b. Relman A. "Self-referral"—What's at stake. *New England Journal of Medicine* (1992) 327:1522–24.

8c. Studdert DM, Mello MM, Brennan TA. Financial conflicts of interest in physicians' relationships with the pharmaceutical industry—self-regulation in the shadow of federal prosecution; *New England Journal of Medicine* (2004) 351:1891–900.

8d. Brennan TA, Rothman DJ, Blank L, et al. Health industry practices that create conflicts of interest *Journal of the American Medical Association* 2006;295:429–433

8e. Berenson A, Pollack A. Doctors reap millions for anemia drugs. *The New York Times* May 9, 2007.

9. Alexander S. They decide who lives, who dies. *Life Magazine* 11/9/62:102–25.

10. Walzer, M. *Spheres of Justice: A Defense of Pluralism and Equality.* New York: Basic Books, 1983.

11. Schneiderman LJ, Jecker NS. *Wrong Medicine: Doctors, Patients, and Futile Treatment.* Baltimore: Johns Hopkins University Press, 1995.

12. Rawls J. *A Theory of Justice.* Cambridge, The Belknap press of Harvard University Press, 1998.

13. Englehart, H.T. *The Foundations of Bioethics.* New York: Oxford University Press, 1996.

14. Daniels N. Justice, Health, and Health Care. In: Rhodes R, Battin MP, Silvers A (Eds.) *Medicine and Social Justice: Essays on the Distribution of Health Care.* New York: Oxford University Press, 2002:8.

15. Zollner H. *Scandanavian Journal of Public Health* (2002) Suppl 59: 6–11.

16. Rhodes R. Justice in medicine and public health. *Cambridge Quarterly of Healthcare Ethics* (2005) 14:13–26.

17. Aaron H. The costs of health care administration in the United States and Canada—questionable answers to a questionable question. *New England Journal of Medicine* (2003) 349:801–3.

18. Illich I, *Medical Nemesis: The Expropriation of Health.* New York: Pantheon Books, 1976: 39–124.

19. Eisenberg DM, Kessler RC, Foster C., et al. Unconventional Medicine in the United States: Prevalence, Costs, and Patterns of Use. *New England Journal of Medicine* (1993) 328:246–52.

19a. Eisenberg DM, Davis RB, Ettner SL, et al. Trends in Alternative Medicine Use in the United States, 1990–1997: Results of a Follow-Up National Survey. *Journal of the American Medical Association* (1998) 280:1569–75.

19b. Eisenberg DM, Kessler RC, Foster C, et al. Unconventional medicine in the United States. Prevalence, costs, and patterns of use. *New England Journal of Medicine* (1993) 328:246–521.

19c. Brody JE. idem., Elder NC, Gillcrist A, Minz R. Use of alternative health care by family practice patients. *Archives of Family Medicine* (1997) 6:181–4.

20. Brody JE. Alternative Medicine Makes Inroads, But Watch Out For Curves. *The New York Times,* April 4, 1998.

21. Root-Bernstein, R., Root-Bernstein, M. *Honey, Mud Maggots, and Other Medical Marvels.* New York: Houghton Mifflin, 1975: 255.

22. Wash. Rev. Code 48.43.045 (1996).

23. Deborah Senn, Insurance Commissioner, Every Category of Provider, Washington Office of Insurance Commissioner Bull. No. 95–9, December 19, 1995.

24. Fisher, R.A. *The Design of Experiments,* 7th ed. New York: Hafner, 1960.

25. Ellis J, Mulligan I, Rowe J, et al. Inpatient General Medicine Is Evidence Based. *The Lancet* (1995) 346: 407–10.

25a. Committee for Evaluating Medical Technologies in Clinical Use, Institute of Medicine, *Assessing Medical Technologies* Washington, D.C.: National Academies Press, 1985.

25b. Gill P, Dowell AC, Neal RD, et al. Evidence Based General Practice: A Retrospective Study of Interventions in One Training Practice, *British Medical Journal* (1996) 312:819–21.

25c. Kamesaki H, Nishizawa K, Michaud GY, et al. Are Therapeutic Decisions Supported by Evidence from Health Care Research? *Archives of Internal Medicine* (1998) 158:1665–68.

26. Chopra, D. *Quantum Healing.* New York: Bantam Books, 1989.

27. *Id.* at 240.

28. Northrup, C., *Women's Bodies, Women's Wisdom.* New York: Bantam Books, 1995.

29. *Id.* at 310.

30. Weil, A., *Spontaneous Healing* New York: Fawcett Columbine, 1995.

31. *Id.* at 235–7.

32. *Id.* at 236.

33. Hilts PJ. Severe Side Effects Are Seen in Experimental AIDS Drug, *The New York Times,* September 27, 1989.

34. Beyerstein BL, Downie S. Naturopathy, *Scientific Review of Alternative Medicine,* 2, no. 1 (1998): 20–8.

34a. Altunc U, Pittler MH, Ernst E. Homeopathy for childhood and adolescence ailments: systematic review of randomized clinical trials. *Mayo Clinic Proceedings* (2007)82(1):69–75.

34b. Ernst E. Are Highly Dilute Homoeopathic Remedies Placebos? *Perfusion* (1998) 11:291–2.

34c. Ernst E, Pittler MH. Letter, Re-Analysis of Previous Meta-Analysis of Clinical Trials of Homeopathy. *Journal of Clinical Epidemiology* (2000) 53:1188.

34d. Linde K, Sholz M, Ramirez G, et al. Impact of Study Quality on Outcome in Placebo-Controlled Trials of Homeopathy. *Journal of Clinical Epidemiology* (1999) 52:631–6.

34e. Vickers AJ. Can Acupuncture Have Specific Effects on Health? A Systematic Review of Acupuncture Antiemesis Trials. *Journal of the Royal Society of Medicine* (1996) 89:303–11.

34f. ter Riet G, Kleiznen J, Knipschild P. Acupuncture and Chronic Pain: A Criteria-Based Meta-Analysis. *Journal of Clinical Epidemiology* (1990) 43:1191–9.

34g. Cherkin DC, Eisenber D, Sherman KJ, et al. Randomized Trial Comparing Traditional Chinese Medical Acupuncture, Therapeutic Massage, and Self-Care Education for Chronic Low Back Pain. *Archives of Internal Medicine* (2001) 161:1081–8.

34h. Allen JJ, Schnyer RN, Chambers AS, Hitt SK, Moreno FA, Manber R. Acupuncture for depression: a randomized controlled trial. *Journal of Clinical Psychiatry* (2006) 67(11):1665–73.

34i. Lim B, Manheimer E, Lao L, et al. Acupuncture for treatment of irritable bowel syndrome. *Cochrane Database Systematic Reviews* (2006) 4:CD005111.

34j. Cheuk DL, Wong V. Acupuncture for epilepsy. *Cochrane Database Systematic Reviews* (2006) 2:CD005062.

34k. Gates S. Smith LA, Foxcroft DR. Auricular acupuncture for cocaine dependence. *Cochrane Database Systematic Reviews* (2006) 1: CD005192.

34l. Zhang SH, Liu M, Asplund K, Li L. Acupuncture for acute stroke. *Cochrane Database Systematic Reviews* (2005) 2:CD003317.

34m. Wu HM, Tang JL, Lin XP, et al. Acupuncture for stroke rehabilitation. *Cochrane Database Systematic Reviews* (2006) 3:CD004131.

34n. Rosa L, Rosa E, Sarner L. A Close Look at Therapeutic Touch. *Journal of the American Medical Association* (1998) 279:1005–10.

34o. Berman BM, Lao L, Langenberg P, Lee WL, Gilpin AM, Hochberg MC. Effectiveness of acupuncture as adjunctive therapy in osteoarthritis of the knee: a randomized, controlled trial. *Annals of Internal Medicine* (2004) 141:901–10.

34p. Vas J, Mendez C, Perez-Milla E, et al. Acupuncture as a complementary therapy to the pharmacological treatment of osteoarthritis of the knee: randomised controlled trial. *British Medical Journal* (2004) 329:1216.

34q. Witt C, Brinkhaus B, Jena S, et al. Acupuncture in patients with osteoarthritis of the knee: a randomised trial. *The Lancet* (2005) 366:136–43.

34r. Scharf HP, Mansmann U, Streitberger K, et al. Acupuncture and knee osteoarthritis: a three-armed randomized trial. *Annals of Internal Medicine* (2006) 145:12–20.

35. 42 U.S.C. 283g(b).

36. Real C.D. Medicine or Medicine Show? Growth of Herbal Remedy Sales Raises Issues About Value. *The New York Times,* July 23, 1998 (quoting David Kessler).

37. Altman LK: Drug mixture curbs HIV in lab, doctors report, but urge caution. *The New York Times,* Feb. 18, 1993, A1.

38. Schneiderman LJ, Jecker NS. Is the treatment beneficial, experimental or futile? *Cambridge Quarterly of Healthcare Ethics* 5:248–56, 1996.

39. Lannin DR, Matthews HF, Mitchell J. Influence of socioeconomic and cultural factors on racial differences in late-stage presentation of breast cancer. *Journal of the American Medical Association* (1998) 278:1801–7.

40. Fisher, R.A. *The Design of Experiments,* 7th ed. New York: Hafner, 1960.

41. Colditz GA, Miller JN, Mosteller F. How Study Design Affects Outcomes in Comparisons of Therapy. *Statistics in Medicine* (1989) 8:441–54.

41a. Schulz KF, Chalmers I, Hayes RJ, et al. Empirical Evidence of Bias: Dimensions of Methodological Quality Associated With Estimates of Treatment Effects in Controlled Trials. *Journal of the American Medical Association,* (1995) 273:408–12.

41b. Khan K, Daya S, and Jadad A. The Importance of Quality of Primary Studies in Producing Unbiased Systematic Reviews. *Archives of Internal Medicine* (1996) 156:661–6.

42. Gifford RH, Feinstein AR. A Critique of Methodology in Studies of Anticoagulant Therapy for Acute Myocardial Infarction. *New England Journal of Medicine* (1969) 280: 351–7.

43. Eddy DM. Investigational Treatments: How Strict Should We Be? *Journal of the American Medical Association,* (1997) 278: 179–85.

44. Stapleton S., Medicine's Chasm, *American Medical News,* June 3, 2002: 29. [quoting A. Sampson]

45. See *id.* (quoting Robert S. Baratz).

46. Crelin, E.S. Chiropractic. In: Stalker D, Glymour C (Eds.). *Examining Holistic Medicine* New York: Prometheus Books, 1989.

46a. Bigos SJ, et al. *Acute Low Back Pain Problems in Adults: Clinical Practice Guideline No. 14,* AHCPR Pub. No. 95–0642. Rockville, Maryland: U.S. Department of Health and Human Services, Public Health Service, Agency for Health Care Policy and Research, 1992.

46b. Shekelle PG, et al. Spinal Manipulation for Low-Back Pain. *Annals of Internal Medicine,* (1992) 117: 590–8.

46c. Coulter I, et al. Congruence Between Decisions to Initiate Chiropractic Spinal Manipulation for Low Back Pain and Appropriateness Criteria in North America. *Annals of Internal Medicine,* (1998) 129: 9–17.

47. Cherkin D.C., et al. A Comparison of Physical Therapy, Chiropractic Manipulation, and Provision of an Educational Booklet for the Treatment of Patients with Low Back Pain. *New England Journal of Medicine* (1998) 339:1021–9.

48. Helms JM. An Overview of Medical Acupuncture. *Alternative Therapies in Health and Medicine* (1998) 4:35–45.

48a. Sherman KJ, Cherkin DC, Hogeboom CJ. The Diagnosis and Treatment of Patients with Chronic Low-Back Pain by Traditional Chinese Medical Acupuncturists. *Journal of Alternative and Complementary Medicine* (2001) 7:641–50.

49. Dimond EG. Acupuncture Anesthesia: Western Medicine and Chinese Traditional Medicine, *Journal of the American Medical Association* (1971) 218:1558–63.

50. Gravitz M.A. Early Uses of Hypnosis as Surgical Anesthesia. *American Journal of Clinical Hypnosis* (1988) 30:201–8.

51. Brown WA. The Placebo Effect. *Scientific American* (1998): 90–5.

51a. de Saintonge MC, Herxheimer A. Harnessing Placebo Effects in Health Care. *The Lancet* (1994) 344:995–8.

51b. Kaptchuk T.J. The Placebo Effect in Alternative Medicine: Can the Performance of a Healing Ritual Have Clinical Significance? *Annals of Internal Medicine* (2002) 136:817–25.

52. Kaptchuk T.J. Acupuncture: Theory, Efficacy, and Practice *Annals of Internal Medicine* (2002) 136:374–83.

53. Gaw AC, Chang LW, Shaw L-C. Efficacy of acupuncture on osteoarthritic pain. A controlled, double-blind study. *New England Journal of Medicine* (1975) 293(8):375–8.

53a. Scharf HP, Mansmann U, Streitberger K, et al. Acupuncture and knee osteoarthritis: a three-armed randomized trial. *Annals of Internal Medicine* (2006) 145:12–20.

53b. Cochrane Handbook for Systematic Reviews of Interventions. http://www.cochrane.org/resources/handbook. Accessed April 30, 2007.

54. Blakeslee S, Placebos Prove So Powerful Even Experts Are Surprised, *The New York Times,* October 13, 1998.

55. Walsh TB, Seidman SN, Sysko R, et al. Placebo Response in Studies of Major Depression: Variable, Substantial, and Growing. *Journal of the American Medical Association,* (2002) 287:1840–7.

56. Schneiderman LJ. Commentary: Bringing Clarity to the Futility Debate: Are the Cases Wrong? *Cambridge Quarterly of Healthcare Ethics* (1998) 7:273–8.

57. Avina RL, Schneiderman LJ. Why Patients Choose Homeopathy. *Western Journal of Medicine* (1978) 128:366–9.

58. Newall, C.A., Anderson, L.A., Phillipson, J.D. *Herbal Medicines: A Guide for Health-Care Professionals.* London: Pharmaceutical Press, 1996.

Appendix

"Unknown Girl in the Maternity Ward"

Child, the current of your breath is six days long.
You lie, a small knuckle on my white bed;
lie, fisted like a snail, so small and strong
at my breast. Your lips are animals; you are fed
with love. At first hunger is not wrong.
The nurses nod their caps; you are shepherded
down starch halls with the other unnested throng
in wheeling baskets. You tip like a cup; your head
moving to my touch. You sense the way we belong.
But this is an institution bed.
You will not know me very long.
The doctors are enamel. They want to know
the facts. They guess about the man who left me,
some pendulum soul, going the way men go
and leave you full of child. But our case history
stays blank. All I did was let you grow.

Now we are here for all the ward to see.
They thought I was strange, although
I never spoke a word. I burst empty
of you, letting you learn how the air is so.
The doctors chart the riddle they ask of me
and I turn my head away. I do not know.
Yours is the only face I recognize.
Bone at my bone, you drink my answers in.
Six times a day I prize
your need, the animals of your lips, your skin
growing warm and plump. I see your eyes
lifting their tents. They are blue stones, they begin
to outgrow their moss. You blink in surprise
and I wonder what you can see, my funny kin,
as you trouble my silence. I am a shelter of lies.
Should I learn to speak again, or hopeless in
such sanity will I touch some face I recognize?
Down the hall the baskets start back. My arms
fit you like a sleeve, they hold
catkins of your willows, the wild bee farms
of your nerves, each muscle and fold
of your first days. Your old man's face disarms
the nurses. But the doctors return to scold
me. I speak. It is you my silence harms.
I should have known; I should have told
them something to write down. My voice alarms
my throat. "Name of father—none." I hold
you and name you bastard in my arms.
And now that's that. There is nothing more

that I can say or lose.
Others have traded life before
and could not speak. I tighten to refuse
your owling eyes, my fragile visitor.
I touch your cheeks, like flowers. You bruise
against me. We unlearn. I am a shore
rocking you off. You break from me. I choose
your only way, my small inheritor
and hand you off, trembling the selves we lose.
Go child, who is my sin and nothing more.

Ann Sexton

"Spring and All"

By the road to the contagious hospital
under the surge of the blue
mottled clouds driven from the
northeast—a cold wind. Beyond, the
waste of broad, muddy fields
brown with dried weeds, standing and fallen

patches of standing water
the scattering of tall trees

All along the road the reddish
purplish, forked, upstanding, twiggy
stuff of bushes and small trees
with dead, brown leaves under them
leafless vines–

Lifeless in appearance, sluggish
dazed spring approaches—

They enter the new world naked,
cold, uncertain of all
save that they enter. All about them
the cold, familiar wind––

Now the grass, tomorrow
the stiff curl of wildcarrot leaf

One by one objects are defined––
It quickens: clarity, outline of a leaf

But now the stark dignity of
entrance––- Still, the profound change
has come upon them: rooted, they
grip down and begin to awaken

William Carlos Williams

Appendix

UCSD HEALTHCARE

UCSD Medical Center Policy & Procedures:
Limitation of Life-Sustaining Treatment

Abstract

This policy and procedure is designed to provide guidelines to follow in those circumstances where the appropriateness of limitation or withdrawal of life-sustaining treatment(s) must be considered. The health care professionals of the UCSD Medical Center are dedicated to the provision of compassionate medical care which benefits patients. The primary principles that should govern decisions to issue withhold or withdraw orders are self-determination, patient welfare, and the futility of medical treatment. It is necessary to establish a policy for withholding and withdrawal of life-sustaining treatments, since patients may not desire such treatments and in certain circumstances such treatments are futile.

Related Policies

UCSDMC MCP-301.8, "Patient Rights";
UCSDMC MCP-305.1, "Advance Directives";
UCSDMC MCP-360.1, "Organ and Tissue Donation
UCSDMC MCP-380.1, "Do Not Attempt to Resuscitate";
Bylaws, Rules, and Regulations of UCSD Medical Staff,
Appendix III-Patient Rights;

Regulatory Reference

California Association of Hospitals and Health Systems,
Chapter 2 and Chapter 4

California Civil Code, 2410–2444: Durable Power of
Attorney for Health Care
California Code of Regulations, Title 22, Licensing and
Certification of Health Facilities and Referral Agencies,
Section 70707
California Health and Safety Code, Sections 7180–7183:
Brain Death, Uniform Determination Act; and Sections
7185–7195: California Natural Death Act.
Emergency Medical Treatment & Active Labor Act
(EMTALA), 42 U.S.C.A 1935dd (West 1992)
Joint Commission on Accreditation of Healthcare Orga-
nizations (JCAHO) Accreditation Manual for Hospitals
Probate Code Section 4753, Request to Forego Resus-
citative Measures
Public Law 101–508: Patient Self Determination Act
Withholding or Withdrawing Life-Sustaining Treatment

I. **PURPOSE**
The purpose of this policy is to provide guidelines regarding the
"Withholding" or "Withdrawal" of Life-Sustaining Treatments
(LST's). [See UCSD Medical Center Guidelines for Comfort
Care, for additional details.]
II. **DEFINITIONS**
    A. **Advance Directive**: An instruction that specifies in ad-
vance the individual's wishes about health care should
the individual become unable to make such decisions.
Examples are an Individual Health Care Instruction, a
Durable Power of Attorney for Health Care valid under
prior law, a Declaration valid under the former Natural Death Act, or a living will. In an Advance Directive, a

patient states choices for medical treatment and/ or designates who should make treatment choices if the person creating the advance directive should lose decision-making capacity.

B. **Durable Power of Attorney for Health Care (DPAHC):** A DPAHC is a type of advance directive that may be set up under the Health Care Decisions Law by which an individual may name someone else (an "agent") to make health care decisions in the event that an individual becomes unable to make such decisions for himself or herself. A DPAHC based upon prior law is still valid if signed after July 1, 2000 only if it is executed on a preprinted form. Under the Health Care Decisions Law, an individual may also include specific instructions regarding which health care treatment(s) should be utilized or omitted in the event of incapacity. The instructions given, if any, are to be followed by the agent. A Power of Attorney may not authorize the attorney In Fact to consent to any of the following on behalf of the principal:

1. Commitment to or placement in a mental health treatment facility;
2. Convulsive treatment
3. Psychosurgery
4. Sterilization;
5. Abortion.

C. **Natural Death Act Declaration (NDAD):** A document in which the patient directs the physician to withhold or withdraw life-sustaining treatment in instances of terminal illness or permanent unconsciousness. Although the law creating the Natural Death Act has been repealed, declarations that were executed before July 1, 2000 remain valid if signed in conformance with the prior law.

D. **Life-Sustaining Treatments (LSTs)**: Those invasive procedures that are necessary to sustain life include feeding tubes, intravenous hydration, and artificial ventilation.

E. **Futile Treatment:** Any treatment that has no realistic chance of providing a benefit that the patient has the capacity to perceive and appreciate, such as merely preserving the physiological functions of a permanent unconscious patient, or has no realistic chance of achieving the medical goal of returning the patient to a level of health that permits survival outside the acute care setting of UCSD Medical Center.

F. **Palliative Care or Comfort Care**: Care whose intent is to relieve suffering and provide for the patient's comfort and dignity. It may include analgesics, narcotics, tranquilizers, local nursing measures, and other treatments including psychological and spiritual counseling. It should be emphasized that although a particular treatment may be futile, palliative or comfort care is never futile. An order to "Withhold" or "Withdraw" LST's does not withhold or withdraw palliative or comfort care.

G. **Responsible Physician**: The attending physician who has primary responsibility for the patient's care, or the senior physician trainee caring for the patient under the instruction of the attending physician.

H. **Attending Physician**: The Attending Physician with primary responsibility for the patient.

I. **Decisionally Capacitated**: A patient is decisionally capacitated to make a health care decision if he or she can understand the condition and the risks and benefits of the recommended treatment and available alternatives (including no treatment), and express a choice. Adults and emancipated minors are presumed to be decisionally capacitated.

J. **Decisionally Incapacitated**: a patient is decisionally incapacitated to make a health care decision if he or she is unable to understand their medical condition, the risk and benefits of recommended treatment and available alternatives.

K. **Surrogate decision-maker**: An individual makinghealth care decisions in substituted judgment on behalf of a decisionally incapacitated patient or an unemancipated minor (usually a parent on behalf of a child). The surrogate must be guided by the patient's desires or, if the patient's desires are unknown, the patient's best interest.

L. **Minor Patients:** Minors are usually considered legally incompetent to make decisions by virtue of their age. However, many minors will be able to understand the nature and consequences of a decision to forgo life-sustaining measures and treatment should not be withdrawn or withheld from a minor unless the minor and the parent(s) or guardian agree. If a conflict exists, the Attending Physician should consult the Ethics Consultation Team and Legal Counsel, as necessary.

III. **POLICY**

It is the policy of UCSD Medical Center to respect the rights of patients (or their surrogate decision-makers) to, with the assistance of their physicians, make informed decisions to refuse life sustaining medical treatment.

IV. **PROCEDURES AND RESPONSIBILITIES**

    A. A discussion concerning the withdrawal or withholding of life-sustaining medical treatment may be initiated by the patient, the patient's surrogate-decision maker, or the Responsible Physician. The Responsible Physician(s) should make every effort to ensure there is adequate communication concerning this decision between the patient or surrogate decision-maker, family members and members of the health care team. The Attending Physician should participate in these discussions, if possible.

    B. **Special Circumstances—Futile Treatment**

        1. A physician has no ethical duty to continue treatment once it has been judged to be futile and ineffective nor to initiate or recommend futile treatment. In such a case, the Attending Physician may write an order within the Attending Orders for Resuscitation Status form when the medical judgment has been made that the patient has reached a state where LST is futile (refer to definition of futile treatment in Section II.E., above).

        2. Any change in the patient's medical condition, such that the patient's prognosis and the likelihood of response to treatment is improved, should be discussed with the patient or the patient's surrogate as appro-

priate, and the Attending Physician should consider whether the treatment plan should be revised.

C. **Dispute Resolution**

1. Dispute resolution is critical in those cases where the patient, family, or legal surrogate and Attending Physician disagree about the futility of continued treatment.

2. An order that "Withholds" or "Withdraws" will not be written within the Attending Orders for Resuscitation Status form and care will not be withheld or withdrawn during the dispute resolution process.

3. Resolution of disagreements may be accomplished through exploration of any of the following mechanisms:

   a. referral to Medical Ethics Committee through the services of the Consultation Team;

   b. transfer of the patient to another Attending Physician;

   c. transfer of the patient to another institution.

D. Once the decision has been made to withhold or withdraw life-sustaining treatments, an order shall be written within the Attending Orders for Resuscitation Status form by the Attending Physician. *If the Attending Physician is not available, a Responsible Physician may write the order within the Attending Orders for Resuscitation Status form after discussing the plan with the attending and having it cosigned by an Attending Physician within 24 hours.*

1. It is the responsibility of the Attending Physician to insure that this order and its meaning are discussed

with all the physicians and nurses caring for the patient.

2. The Attending Physician is responsible for the judgments relevant to the forms of treatment that are to be withheld or withdrawn.

3. The Attending Physician shall write or countersign the note of a resident or fellow discussing the withhold or withdrawal of care decision.

   a. the diagnosis and prognosis that supports any physician determination of futility described under Section II.D.;

   b. the decisions and recommendations of the treatment team and consultants;

   c. an assessment of the patient's competency; and the competent patient's wishes. In cases involving incompetent patients, the expression of those wishes by the patient's surrogate should be recorded, including the nature of the relationship.

5. It is the responsibility of the Attending Physician who is transferring care of the patient to another Attending Physician to ensure that the accepting Attending Physician is provided with information concerning the withdrawal or withholding of LSTs.

6. The "Withhold" or "Withdraw" order should be under regular periodic review by the Attending Physician to insure the order remains current and consistent with the patient's desires, medical condition and prognosis.

7. Attending Physicians assuming the care of patients with "Withhold" or "Withdraw" orders will con-

tinue those orders or will document why they should change.

8. Attending Physicians and health care professionals who feel that they cannot carry out a "Withhold" or "Withdraw" order may request a change of assignment providing this does not result in abandonment of the patient.

Index

215

Index